T0043520

Praise for Anthony De Mello

"Even though Anthony De Mello's approach reaches such vast dimensions, it is one he made available to anyone willing to enter this work of the soul."

—**Thomas Moore**, author of *Care of the Soul*

"Anthony De Mello is one of my favorite enlightened guys."
—**Adyashanti**, Open Gate Sangha and author of *The End of Your World*

"I will never forget the feeling of liberation; the sense he made of spirituality, of prayer, of the meaning of life; his humor; his marvelous storytelling. And it was all done in such a personal style."

—**J. Francis Stroud**, S.J. author of *Praying Naked*

"This is your wake-up call! You may not have even realized you were sleepwalking. Most of us *are* most of the time. . . . Anthony De Mello [is] telling you gently but firmly, 'It's time to get up now.'"

—**Charles Osgood**, former host of *CBS Sunday Morning*

STOP FIXING YOURSELF

Wake Up, All Is Well

STOP FIXING YOURSELF

Wake Up, All Is Well

ANTHONY DE MELLO

Edited by Don Joseph Goewey

BEYOND WORDS
Portland, Oregon

BEYOND WORDS

1750 S.W. Skyline Blvd, Suite 20
Portland, Oregon 97221-2543
503-531-8700 / 503-531-8773 fax
www.beyondword.com

CONTENTS

NOTE FROM THE EDITOR

Years ago, I came across the work of Anthony (Tony) De Mello and it helped me immensely. It reinforced in me a profound way of being, but, like so many of us, I only applied it sporadically. Then, as fate would have it, I was invited to join the De Mello Spirituality Center to assist in its mission to bring Tony's work even further out into the world. It afforded me the opportunity to delve deeply into Tony's spiritual philosophy and approach and to understand its power to open our eyes to a profound truth: namely, that *all is well*. Though everything remains a mess, *all is well*. Given that this is true, it follows that we are all OK, with really nothing to fix or change in ourselves. We are not a problem to be solved. If there is a problem, it is that we have not yet understood this. As a result, we continue being anxious, insecure, fearful, resentful, unforgiving, and aggressive. In short, we suffer, while, as Tony asserts, all around us there is a divinity within easy grasp that would make our lives meaningful, beautiful, and rich, if we would only discover it. Then these things we struggle to fix would change all by themselves. That's *grace*, which is what Tony is pointing to, and grace is at the heart of this collection of his writings.

What Tony did for the world was to show how simple this discovery can be. It just requires being fundamentally aware of what is going on inside us until awareness wakes us up to the truth, which awareness is guaranteed to do.

What Tony did for me was to help me understand the way our society programs people to habitually undermine their own happiness and then to blame themselves for it. Again, like so many of us, I was raised on the old formula that had me believing that if I worked hard, success would follow, and then happiness would come out of that. So, I followed the prescription. I worked hard on changing myself and my situation. Then, around the time I happened onto Tony's work, I came to the realization that this formula was not the way happiness happened. It actually blocked happiness by producing a chronic condition of always seeking and never finding. Ironically, the first time I opened one of Tony's books at random, I landed on a page which posed the very question that drives this old formula:

What do you need to do to change yourself?

Tony's answer to this question astounded me.

He said, you don't have to do anything; it's enough for you to simply be watchful and awake. Awareness, he said, releases reality to change you. He asserted that by simply being aware, all that is false and neurotic within you will drop and your eyes will open to the divinity surrounding you. You will suddenly see that all *is* well;

that you are already happy, right now, and always have been; that you are already at peace right now, and always were, but you just did not know it.

That's where life becomes beautiful, he said, and all we have to do is to be aware of our reactions—positive and negative—and let *grace* do the work of restoring us to the experience we were born to have. Do that, Tony said, and you will make the biggest discovery in your life.

Beauty and happiness are what every human being wants, so, I recommitted myself to becoming more aware as Tony described. For two weeks I observed the thoughts, feelings, and beliefs that generated the way I reacted to people and events (which mostly were stressful), and how those reactions distorted the way I saw the world. Then one fine day, I experienced the big discovery Tony was pointing to. I discovered that, in that exact moment, I had everything I needed to be happy. The only reason I was ever unhappy or discontent was because I was focused on what I did not have. That discovery happened in New York at Grand Central Station during rush hour. I was late and had missed my train. I was angry with myself, but I managed to step back into awareness. As I stood in the crowd, I observed my angst rattling my nerves, agitating me with anger and self-judging thoughts that were turning into projections, looking to blame someone else. But as I allowed my reaction to be the way it was, getting clear that the reaction was in me and not reality, and refraining from judging myself for having judged myself, the reaction gradually passed. All at once, I was aware of the splendor of Grand Central Station and dazzled by the immense human drama happening all around me. Something wonderful awakened in me and I felt love for every single person in that crowd. It was like a veil had been lifted, revealing the beauty and joy that was always there, free for the taking. Awareness had set me free.

That freedom is what Anthony De Mello is pointing to. Our world needs it more than ever, and you can find your way to freedom in this book.

—Don Joseph Goewey,
executive director of the De Mello Spirituality Center

FOREWORD

There is a Tony De Mello story that provides the perfect introduction to this book:

> The disciple asks the master, "What is more important, meditation or action?"
>
> "Neither," says the master. "Seeing is what's important."
>
> "But we see all the time," countered the disciple. "See that the golden necklace you so ardently desire is already hanging around your neck.
>
> "See that those snakes you imagine biting at your ankles are only harmless pieces of rope. See what's really there."

If you let that story roll around in your brain while reading this book, you will be able to *stop fixing yourself.* The stories, narratives, and meditations in each section provide you effortless and enjoyable moments of awareness.

Much as a flame disintegrates a piece of cellophane, these moments will gently dissolve the false, neurotic programming within you.

My life changed is the most frequent sentence uttered by those who have discovered the De Mello *magic*. Though everything around you may be a mess, you are just fine. There is no need to go anywhere else. In the present moment happiness arises all by itself. So it is with this book. You don't have to do anything more. Just let it speak to you.

—Desmond Towey,
trustee of the De Mello Spirituality Center

INTRODUCTION

As You Read This Book

Spirituality means waking up. Some of us get woken up by the harsh realities of life. We suffer so much that we wake up. Other people keep bumping into life again and again. They still go on sleepwalking. They never wake up. Tragically, it never occurs to them that there may be another way. It never occurs to them that there may be a better way. Still, if you haven't been bumped sufficiently by life, and you haven't suffered enough, then there is another way: to *listen*. I don't mean you have to agree with what I'm stating. That wouldn't be listening. It doesn't matter whether you agree or not, because agreement and disagreement have to do with words and concepts and theories. They don't have anything to do with truth. Truth is never expressed in words. Truth is sighted suddenly, as a result of a certain attitude. So you could be disagreeing with me and still sight the truth. But there has to be an attitude of openness, of willingness to discover something new. That's important—not your agreeing with me or disagreeing with me. After all, most of what I'm presenting here is really theories. No theory adequately covers reality. I can speak to you, not of the truth, but of obstacles to the truth. Those I can describe. I cannot describe the truth. No one can. All I can do is give you a description of your falsehoods, so that you can drop them. All I can do for you is challenge your beliefs and the belief system that makes you unhappy. All I can do for you is help you to unlearn. That's what learning is all about where spirituality is concerned: unlearning, unlearning almost everything you've been taught. A willingness to unlearn, to listen.

Ask yourself as you read this book, "Am I listening, as most people do, in order to confirm what I already think?" Observe your reactions as you read. You'll frequently be startled or shocked or scandalized or irritated or annoyed or frustrated. Or you'll be saying, "Great!" But are you listening for what will confirm what you already think? Or are you listening in order to discover something new? That is important. It is difficult for sleeping people. Jesus proclaimed the good news yet he was rejected. Not because it wasn't good, but because it was new. We hate the new, and the sooner we face up to that fact, the better. We don't want new things, particularly when they're disturbing, particularly when they involve change. Most particularly, if they involve saying, "I was wrong."

I remember meeting an eighty-seven-year-old Jesuit who attended a workshop I'd given. "I should have heard you speak sixty years ago," he said. "You know something. I've been wrong all my life." God, to listen to that! It's like beholding one of the wonders of the world.

That, dear reader, is *faith*! An openness to the truth, no matter what the consequences, no matter where it leads you and when you don't even know where it's going to lead you. That's faith—not belief—but faith. Your beliefs give you a lot of security, but faith is insecurity. You don't know. You're ready to follow and you're open, you're wide open! You're ready to listen. And, mind you, being open does not mean being gullible. It doesn't mean swallowing whatever the speaker is saying. Oh no. You've got to challenge everything I'm saying. But challenge it from an attitude of openness, not from an attitude of stubbornness. And challenge it all. Recall those lovely words of Buddha when he said, "Monks and scholars must not accept my words out of respect but must analyze them the way a goldsmith analyzes gold—by cutting, scraping, rubbing, melting." When you do that, you're listening. You've taken another major step toward awakening.

The Parable of the Sannyasi

Sometimes a simple story can say more than a whole day at a retreat. That is because stories speak to the depths within us. I want to tell you one of my favorite stories that speaks to the depth of me. It has to do with true happiness.

It is a story of a villager in India who happens upon a sannyasi. A sannyasi is a wandering mendicant who, having attained enlightenment, understands that the whole world is his home and the sky is his roof. He knows that God is his father, and God will look after him, so he moves from place to place the way you and I move from one room of our home to another.

"I cannot believe this," the villager exclaimed to the sannyasi when their paths crossed.

The sannyasi responded, "What is it you cannot believe?"

"I had a dream about you last night," the villager said. "I dreamed that the Lord Vishnu said to me, 'Tomorrow morning, you will leave the village, and you will run into a wandering sannyasi.' And here you are!"

"What else did the Lord Vishnu say to you?" the sannyasi asked.

"He said that you possess a precious stone and that, should you give it to me, its value will make me the richest man in the world," the villager said. "So—do you have such a stone?"

The sannyasi began rummaging through his knapsack and, after a moment, pulled out an object.

"Would this be the stone you saw in your dream?" said the sannyasi, handing the stone to the villager.

The villager could not believe his eyes. It was the same stone—a diamond as big as his fist. He held the diamond in his two hands with great care.

"Could I have this stone?" he asked.

"Of course," the sannyasi said. "Please, take it. I found it in the forest, and you're welcome to it."

The villager took the diamond and went to sit under a tree on the outskirts of the village. He held the diamond close to his heart, and he experienced great joy.

Now, this is the kind of joy most people feel the day they get something they really want. Have you ever stopped to ask how long that kind of joy lasts? You got the girl you wanted, right? You got the boy you wanted. You got that car. You got the degree. You were at the top of your class. You got what you thought was your dream job, right? How long does that joy last? How many seconds? How many minutes?

Eventually, you grew tired of what you got—didn't you?—and soon you were off looking for something else. Understanding this truth is more valuable than studying the Scriptures because what good is it to you to study the Scriptures if you've not understood this? What good is it if you've not understood what it means to live, and to be free, and to be spiritual?

So, the villager sat under a tree all day, clutching his diamond, and he became immersed in thought. And toward evening, he returned to the place where the sannyasi was meditating, and he gave him back the diamond.

"I've decided that this wasn't what I was looking for," he said. "But may I ask you to do me one more favor?"

"What is it?" asked the sannyasi.

"Could you give me the inner richness that makes it possible for you to so easily give away this thing that would have made you the richest man in the world?"

PART ONE

NOW IS THE TIME

"Can you imagine how liberating it is to never be disillusioned again, to never be disappointed again? You'll never feel let down again. Never feel rejected. Want to wake up? You want happiness? You want freedom? Here it is: Drop your false ideas."

The Divine Flame of Discontent

Sooner or later, there arises in every human heart the desire for holiness, spirituality, God—call it what you will. One hears mystics speak of a divinity all around us that is within our grasp, that would make our lives meaningful and beautiful and rich, if we could only discover it. But look at the heartache everywhere, look at the loneliness, look at the fear, the confusion, the conflict in the hearts of people. Inner conflict. Outer conflict.

Have you ever felt disgusted with life, sick at heart of constantly running away from fears and anxieties, weary of your begging rounds, exhausted from being dragged about helplessly by your attachments and addictions?

Have you ever felt the utter meaninglessness of working for a degree, finding a job, then settling down to a life of boredom? Or, if you are an achiever, settling down to a life of emotional turmoil caused by the things that you are chasing after?

If you have—and is there a single human being who hasn't?— the divine flame of discontent has arisen within your heart. Now is the time to fan it before it gets stamped out by the routine chores of life. Now is the Holy Season when you simply must find the time to get away and look at your life, allowing the flame to grow as you look, refusing to let anything distract you from this task.

3

SEARCH INSIDE YOURSELF

Contrary to what your culture and religion have taught you, nothing—but absolutely nothing of the world—can make you happy. The moment you see that, you will stop moving from one job to another, one friend or lover to another, one place, one spiritual technique, one guru to another. None of these things can give you a single minute of happiness. They can only offer you a temporary thrill, a pleasure, that initially grows in intensity then turns into pain if you lose them and boredom if you keep them.

Think of the numberless persons and things that so excited you in the past. What happened? In every single instance, they ended up causing you suffering or boredom—did they not? It is absolutely essential that you understand this because, until you do, there is no question of your ever finding the Kingdom of Joy.

Search within your heart, and you will find something there that will make it possible for you to understand—a spark of disenchantment and discontent. If fanned into flame, it will become a raging forest fire that will burn up the whole of the illusory world you are living in, thereby unveiling to your wondering eyes the kingdom that you have always unsuspectingly lived in.

People have a vague idea as to what this thing is, and they read books and consult gurus in an attempt to find out what they must do to gain that elusive thing called Holiness or Spirituality. They pick up all sorts of methods, techniques, spiritual exercises, and formulas. Then, after years of fruitless striving, they become discouraged and confused and wonder what went wrong. Most often, people blame themselves. They think, "If I'd only practiced those techniques more regularly, or, if I had been more fervent or more generous, then I might have made it." But made *what*? They have no clear idea as to what the holiness or enlightenment that they seek *is*—but they certainly know that their lives are still unhappy. They still become anxious, insecure, and fearful; resentful and unforgiving; grasping, ambitious, and manipulative of people. Once again, they throw themselves with renewed vigor into what they think they need to do to fix themselves and attain their goal.

STOP FIXING YOURSELF

Suppose there is a way of getting rid of all of that? Suppose there is a way to stop that tremendous drain of energy, health, and emotion that comes from such conflicts and confusion. Would you want that? Suppose there is a way that we would truly love one another, and be at peace, be at love.

People ask me all the time, what do I need to do to change myself? If you are one of those people, I've got a big surprise for you! You don't have to do anything. In fact, the more you do, the worse it gets. All you have to do is understand. The trouble with most people is that they're busy trying to fix things in themselves that they really don't understand.

Stop fixing yourself. You're OK. Don't interfere. Don't fix anything. Simply watch. Observe. These things in you that you struggle to fix just need to be understood. If you understood them, they would change.

Most people have never stopped to consider this simple fact: Their efforts are going to get them nowhere. Their efforts will only make things worse, as things become worse when you use fire to put out fire. Effort does not lead to growth. Effort, whatever the form it takes, whether it be willpower, habit, a technique, or a spiritual exercise, does not lead to change. At best, effort leads to repression and a covering over of the root problem. Effort may change the outward behavior, but it does not change the inner person.

Just think what kind of a mentality it betrays when you ask, "What must I do to get holiness? What sacrifices must I make? What discipline must I undertake? What meditation must I practice in order to get it?" Think of a man who wants to win the love of a woman and attempts to improve his appearance, build his body, change his behavior, and practice techniques to charm her. And so it is with spirituality and holiness. It is not what you do that brings it to you. What matters is what you are and what you become.

ALL IS WELL

All mystics—no matter what the theology and no matter what the religion—are unanimous on one thing: all is well.

Though everything is a mess, all is well. They say you are already happy right now, though you don't know it.

Strange paradox, to be sure.

Tragically, most people never get to see that all is well because they are asleep, even though they don't know it. They are having a nightmare. They don't understand the loveliness and the beauty of this thing we call human existence.

Put On a New Mind

Wake up! Life is a banquet; the tragedy is that most people are starving to death. It's like the people who were stuck on a raft off the coast of Brazil, perishing from thirst. They had no idea that the water they were floating on was fresh water. The river was emptying into the sea with such force that it reached into waters a couple of miles out. They had freshwater right where they were—but they had no idea.

In the same way, we're surrounded with joy, happiness, and love, but most people have no idea about it whatsoever. The reason? They're brainwashed. The reason? They're hypnotized. They're asleep. It's like a stage magician who hypnotizes someone so that the person sees what is not there and does not see what is there.

You've Been Programmed to Be Unhappy

Has it ever struck you that you have been programmed by society to be unhappy, and so, no matter what you do to become happy, you are bound to fail? Most people are so brainwashed that they do not even realize how unhappy they are. It's only when they make contact with joy that they understand how depressed they have been.

If you wish to be happy, the first thing you need isn't effort or even goodwill or good desires. You need a clear understanding of exactly how you have been programmed. This is what happened to you:

First your society and your culture taught you to believe that you would not be happy without certain persons and certain things. Just take a look around you. Everywhere you look, people have built their lives on the unquestioned belief that without money, power, success, approval, a good reputation, love, friendship, spirituality, or God, they cannot be happy.

What is your particular combination?

Once you swallowed this belief, you naturally developed an attachment to some person or thing you were convinced that, without it, you could not be happy. Then followed your efforts to acquire your precious thing or person, to cling to it once it was acquired, and to fight off every possibility of losing it.

This finally led you to abject emotional dependence so that the object of your attachment had the power to thrill you when you attained it, to make you anxious lest you be deprived of it, and make you miserable when you lost it.

Stop for a moment and contemplate in horror the endless list of attachments that you have become a prisoner to. Think of concrete things and persons, not abstractions. Once your attachment had you in its grip, you began to strive with every waking minute of your life to rearrange the world around you so that you could attain and maintain the objects of your attachment.

This is an exhausting task. It leaves you little energy for the business of living and enjoying life fully. It is also an impossible task in an ever-changing world that you simply are not able to control. So, instead of living a life of serenity and fulfillment, you are doomed to a life of frustration, anxiety, worry, insecurity, suspense, and tension. For a few fleeting moments, the world does indeed yield to your efforts and rearranges itself to suit your desires. Then you experience a flash of pleasure and become happy, briefly. But it isn't happiness at all because it is accompanied by the underlying fear that at any moment this world of things and people that you have painstakingly put in place will slip out of your control and let you down. And sooner or later, it will.

You've Been Trained to Upset Yourself

If you take a look at the way you have been put together and the way you function, you will find that inside your head there is a whole program stamped into you, a set of demands about how the world should be, how you should be, and what you should want.

Who is responsible for the programming?

Not you. It isn't really you who decided even such basics as your wants, desires, and so-called needs, your values, your tastes, and your attitudes. It was your parents, your society, your culture, your religion, and your past experiences that fed the operating instructions into your computer. Now, however old you are or wherever you go, your computer goes along with you and is active and operating at each conscious moment of the day. It is imperiously insisting that its demands be met by life, by people, and by you. If the demands are met, the computer allows you to be peaceful and happy. If they are not met, even though it is no fault of yours, the computer generates negative emotions that cause you to suffer.

In short, you've been trained to upset yourself. For instance, when other people don't live up to your computer's expectations, it torments you with frustration, anger, or bitterness. When things are not under your control, or the future is uncertain, your computer insists that you experience anxiety, tension, or worry. Then you expend a lot of energy coping with these negative emotions by expending even more energy trying to rearrange the world around you so that the demands of your computer will be met. If that happens, you will be granted a measure of precarious peace; it's precarious because at any moment, some trifle—a plane delay, a smart phone that doesn't work, an email that hasn't arrived, a spot on your tie or blouse, you name it—is going to be out of conformity with your computer's programming, and the computer will insist that you become upset again. These things depend on the criteria society establishes; they depend on your conditioning.

It becomes a way of life. It is a pathetic existence that is constantly at the mercy of things and people as you try desperately to make life conform to your computer's demands so that you can enjoy the only peace you can ever know—a temporary respite from negative emotions.

You've Been Infected with Attachments

Take a look at the society we live in. It is rotten to the core, infected with attachments. What is an attachment? An attachment is an emotional state of clinging caused by the belief that without some particular thing or some person you cannot be happy.

How is an attachment formed? First, there's contact with something that gives you pleasure: a car, an attractively advertised modern appliance, a word of praise, or a person's company. Then comes the desire to hold on to it and to repeat the gratifying sensation that the thing or person caused you. Finally comes the conviction that you will not be happy without that person or thing for you have equated the pleasure it brings you with happiness.

If you look carefully, you will see that the one and only thing that causes unhappiness is attachment. It is composed of two elements, one positive and the other negative. The positive element is the flash of pleasure and excitement, the thrill that you experience when you get what you are attached to. The negative element is the sense of threat and tension that always accompanies the attachment.

Think of someone gobbling up food in a concentration camp. With one hand, he brings the food to his mouth; with the other hand, he protects it from neighbors who will grab it from him the moment he lowers his guard. There you have the perfect image of the attached person.

Do you have any attachments to people or things that you falsely believe you could not be happy without? Make a list of them right now. Spend some time seeing each thing you cling to for what it really is—a nightmare that causes you excitement and pleasure on the one hand but also worry, insecurity, tension, anxiety, fear, and unhappiness on the other. Father and mother? Nightmare. Wife and children, brothers and sisters? Nightmare. All your possessions? Nightmare. Your life as it is now? Nightmare. Every single thing you cling to and have convinced yourself you cannot live without? Nightmare.

There are even people who dread to challenge and lose a pet theory, ideology, or belief they are attached to. Do you want to know how to measure the degree of rigidity and deadness attachments cause? Observe the amount of pain you experience when you lose a cherished idea, person, or thing. The pain and the grief betray your clinging, do they not? That is why, when life bursts in to shatter your illusions, you experience so much pain. An attachment, by its very nature, makes you vulnerable to emotional turmoil and is always threatening to shatter your peace.

So how can you expect an attached person to enter that ocean of happiness called the Kingdom of God? As well as you can expect a camel to pass through the eye of a needle!

Anyone who stops clinging to brothers, sisters, father, mother, children, land, or houses is repaid a hundred times over and gains eternal life. Then you will so easily take leave of your possessions, that is, you will stop clinging, and you will have destroyed clinging's capacity to hurt you. Then, at last, you will experience that mysterious state that cannot be described or uttered—the state of abiding happiness and peace.

Why You Are Afraid and Anxious

Whenever you are anxious and afraid, it is because you might lose—or fail to get—the object of your attachment, isn't it? And any time you feel jealous, isn't it because someone might make off with what you are attached to? Almost all of your anger comes from someone standing in the way of your attachment, doesn't it? See how paranoid you become when your attachment is threatened? You can't think objectively. Your whole vision becomes distorted, doesn't it?

Every time you feel bored, isn't it because you are not getting a sufficient supply of what you believe will make you happy? Of what you are attached to? And when you are depressed and miserable, the cause is there for everyone to see: Life is not giving you what you have convinced yourself you can't be happy without.

The One and Only Thing
You Need to Do

Hardly anyone has been told the following truth: In order to be genuinely happy, there is one and only one thing you need to do—get deprogrammed and get rid of those attachments.

When people stumble upon this self-evident truth, they become terrified at the thought of the pain involved in dropping their attachments. But the process is not a painful one at all. On the contrary, getting rid of attachments is a perfectly delightful task, that is, if the instrument you use to rid yourself of them is not willpower or renunciation, but sight.

All you need to do is open your eyes and see that you do not really need the object of your attachment at all—that you were programmed, brainwashed into thinking that you could not be happy or you could not live without that particular person or thing.

Remember how heartbroken you once were—how you were certain you never would be happy again—because you lost someone or something that was precious to you? But then what happened? Time passed, and you learned to get on pretty well, didn't you? That should have alerted you to the falseness of your belief, to the trick your programmed mind was playing on you.

An attachment is not a fact. It is a belief, a fantasy, in your head, acquired through programming. If that fantasy did not exist inside your head, you would not be attached. You would love things and people, and you would enjoy them thoroughly, but on a nonattachment basis. As a matter of fact, is there any other way to really enjoy something?

Take a moment now to review all of your attachments. To each person or thing that comes to mind, say: "I am not really attached to you at all. I am merely deluding myself into the belief that without you I will not be happy." Do this honestly and see the change that comes about within you.

When you're ready to exchange your illusions for reality, when you're ready to exchange your dreams for facts, that's when life finally becomes meaningful. That's where life becomes beautiful. Can you imagine how liberating it is to never be disillusioned again, to never be disappointed again? You'll never feel let down again. Never feel rejected. Want to wake up? You want happiness? You want freedom? Here it is: Drop your false ideas.

THE FALSE BELIEFS

What are the false beliefs that block you from happiness?

The first false belief: You cannot be happy without the things that you are attached to and that you consider so precious.

This is false. There is not a single moment in your life when you do not have everything that you need to be happy. Think about that for a minute. The reason you are unhappy is that you are focusing on what you do not have rather than on what you have right now.

Another false belief: Happiness is in the future.

Not true. Right here and now you are happy, and you do not know it because your false beliefs and your distorted perceptions have gotten you caught up in fears, anxieties, attachments, conflicts, guilt, and a host of games that you are programmed to play.

If you see through this illusion, you would realize that you are happy and did not know it.

Another false belief: *Happiness will come if you manage to change the situation you are in and the people around you.*
It's not true. You stupidly squander so much energy trying to rearrange the world. If changing the world is your vocation in life, go right ahead and change it, but do not harbor the illusion that it will make you happy.

What makes you happy or unhappy is not the world and the people around you, but the thinking in your head. Might as well search for an eagle's nest on the bed of an ocean—a search for happiness in the world outside you will be just as successful.

If it is happiness that you seek, you can stop wasting your energy trying to cure your baldness, building up an attractive body, or changing your residence, your job, your community, your lifestyle, or even your personality. Do you realize that you could change every one of these things—you could have the finest looks, the most charming personality, and the most pleasant of surroundings—and still be unhappy? Deep down, you know this is true. But still you waste your effort and energy trying to get what you know cannot make you happy.

Another false belief: *If all of your desires are fulfilled, you will finally be happy.*

Not true. In fact, it is these very desires and attachments that make you tense, frustrated, nervous, insecure, and fearful. Look at your list of your attachments and desires and to each of them, say these words: "Deep down in my heart, I know that even after I have gotten you, I will not get happiness." Ponder the truth of these words. The fulfillment of desire can, at the most, bring flashes of pleasure and excitement. Don't mistake them for happiness.

THE SYMPHONY OF LIFE

You also falsely think that your fears protect you, that your beliefs have made you what you are, and that your attachments make your life exciting and secure. You fail to see that they are actually a screen between you and life's symphony. It is quite impossible, of course, to be fully conscious of every note in life's symphony. But if your spirit becomes unclogged and your senses open, you will begin to perceive things as they really are. You will begin to interact with reality, and you will be entranced by the harmonies of the universe. Then, you will understand what God is—for you will at last know what love is.

Look at it this way: You don't see persons and things as they are; you see them as you are. If you wish to see them as they are, you must attend to your attachments and the fears that they generate. It is these attachments and fears that will decide what you notice about life and what you block out. Then, whatever you notice commands your attention, and since your looking has been selective, you have an illusory vision of the things and people around you. The more you look with this distorted version, the more you become convinced that it is the true picture of the world—and your attachments and fears will continue to process incoming data in a way that reinforces your picture.

This is how your beliefs originate: they are fixed, unchanging ways of looking at a reality that is not fixed and unchanging at all, but constantly moving and changing. So, it is no longer the real world that you interact with and love, but a world created by your head. It is only when you drop your beliefs, fears, and the attachments that breed them that you will be freed from the insensitivity that makes you so deaf and blind to yourself and the world.

Think of yourself listening to an orchestra, and the sound of the drum is so loud that nothing else can be heard. To enjoy the symphony, you must be responsive to every instrument in the orchestra. To be in the state called love, you must be sensitive to the uniqueness and beauty of every single thing and person around you. You can hardly be said to love what you do not even notice; and if you notice only a few beings to the exclusion of others, that is not love at all. For love excludes no one at all; it embraces the whole of life. Love listens to the symphony as a whole, not to just one or the other of the musical instruments.

Stop for a moment now to consider how your attachments drain life's symphony of sound for you no less than a politician's attachment to power or the businessman's attachment to money have deafened them to the melody of life.

Programmed Not to Question the Programming

We have been programmed to not suspect or doubt. We have been programmed to trust the assumptions that have been put into us by our tradition, culture, society, and religion. That's another part of society's brainwashing. If we are attached to power, money, property, fame, and success—if we seek these things as if our happiness depended on them—we will be considered a productive member of society, dynamic, and hardworking. In other words, if we pursue these things with a driving ambition that destroys the symphony of our life and makes us hard and cold and insensitive to others and to ourselves, society will look upon us as a dependable citizen, and our relatives and friends will be proud of the status that we have achieved.

How many so-called respectable people do you know who have retained the gentle sensitivity of love, which only unattachment can offer? They look for what fosters or threatens them and turn a blind eye to the rest of life. They won't be interested in the rest any more than the avaricious businessman is interested in anything that does not involve the making of money. Think of a politician who has convinced himself he will not be happy unless he gets political power. His quest for power coarsens his sensitivity to the rest of life, and he barely has time for his family and friends. Suddenly, he perceives and reacts to all human beings in terms of the support or threat that they are to his ambition. And those who can neither threaten nor support, he does not even notice. If, in addition to his craving for power, he has an attachment to other things, such as sex or money, the poor man will become so selective in his perceptions that he could almost be said to be blind. Everyone sees it except the man himself. It is the condition that leads to the rejection of the Messiah, the rejection of truth and beauty and goodness because one has become too blind to perceive them.

A loving heart is sensitive to the whole of life—to all persons. A loving heart doesn't harden itself to any person or thing. There is nothing so clear-sighted as love. Love entails clarity of perception and objectivity. But the moment you become attached, you block out many other things. You've got eyes only for the object of your attachment while your heart has hardened.

You can keep as many attachments as you want, but for each attachment you pay a price in lost happiness. Think of it this way: The nature of attachments is such that, even if you satisfy many of them in the course of a single day, the one attachment that was not satisfied will prey upon your mind and make you unhappy. There is no way to win the battle of attachments, yet you have been trained to blame yourself and to be blind to your unhappiness as a result of your cultural and inherited programming.

You're not to blame. You're not doing this deliberately. Who would deliberately cause suffering for themselves? Unhappiness comes from your programming.

So, should you blame your programming? No. You're not blaming your programming; you're understanding that the programming is where the pain comes from and, as a result of understanding, you can be freed from it.

The Kingdom of Joy

To find the Kingdom of Joy is the easiest thing in the world but also the most difficult. It's easy because it is all around you and within you, and all you have to do is reach out and take possession of it. It's difficult because, if you wish to possess the Kingdom, you can possess nothing else. That is, you must drop all inward leaning on any person or thing and forever withdraw from them the power to thrill you, excite you, or give you a feeling of security or well-being.

But people still go on sleepwalking. Waking up is unpleasant. We are nice and comfortable in bed; it's irritating to be woken up. That's the reason the wise guru does not attempt to wake people up.

The first step to waking up is to be honest enough to admit to yourself that you don't like it. You don't want to be happy. What you want is for someone to mend your broken toys.

"Give me back my lover." "Give me back my job." "Give me back my money." "Give me back my reputation, my success."

We are told by our society and our culture that happiness is a thing, such as a smooth complexion or a holiday resort. But happiness isn't a thing, yet we have subtle ways of making our happiness depend on things within us and outside of us.

We don't want to be happy. We're programmed to want other things. To put it more accurately: We don't want to be unconditionally happy. "I'm ready to be happy provided I have this and that and the other thing." It is the same as saying to someone, even God, "You are my happiness. If I don't get you, I refuse to be happy."

If we want to come awake—which is the same thing as saying, "If we want to love, if we want freedom, if we want joy and peace and spirituality"—this is the first thing we need to understand.

Want a little test to prove that you don't want to be happy? Think of someone you love very much—someone you're close to, someone who is precious to you—and, in your mind, say to that person: "I'd rather have happiness than have you." Then, see what happens.

Did you feel selfish when you said it?

We've been brainwashed into thinking, "How could I be so selfish?"

But look at who's being selfish. Imagine somebody saying to you, "How could you be so selfish that you'd choose happiness over me?" Wouldn't you feel like responding, "Pardon me, but how could you be so selfish that you would demand I choose you above my own happiness?!"

Driving with the Brakes On

Society and culture determine what it means to be a success and drill it into our heads, day and night. Stop to consider this: Having a good job or being famous or having a great reputation has absolutely nothing to do with happiness or success. Nothing! It is totally irrelevant. Do you want to be one of those people who society says made it? Made what?! Made asses of themselves because they drained all their energy getting something that was worthless. They're frightened and confused. Do you call that a success? They are controlled and manipulated. They are miserable. They don't enjoy life. They are constantly tense and anxious. Do you call that human?

If you contemplate this long enough, you will experience a disgust so deep that you will instinctively fling every attachment away as you would toss away a serpent that has settled on you. You will revolt and break loose from this putrid culture that is based on acquisitiveness and attachment, anxiety and greed, and on the hardness and insensitivity of nonlove.

Wake up! You don't need this. It's wasting your life. You can be blissfully happy without your attachments. People think that if they had no cravings, they would be like deadwood, but in fact they would lose their tension. If you get rid of your fear of failure and drop your tensions about succeeding, you will be yourself. You will be relaxed. You won't be driving with your brakes on. That's what would happen.

There's a lovely account from Tranxu, a great Chinese sage, that goes: "When the archer shoots for no particular prize, he has all his skills. When he shoots to win a brass buckle, he is already nervous. When he shoots for a gold prize, he goes blind, sees two targets, and is out of his mind. His skill has not changed, but the prize divides him. He cares! He thinks more of winning than of shooting, and the need to win drains him of power."

Isn't that an image of most people?

When you're living for nothing, you've got all your skills, you've got all your energy, you're relaxed, and you don't care. It doesn't matter to you whether you win or lose. Now there's human living for you. That's what life is all about.

The mystics and the prophets didn't bother one bit about honor. Honor or disgrace meant nothing to them. They were living in another world, the world of the awakened. Success or failure meant nothing to them.

THE CONTRAST OF WORLDLY FEELINGS TO SOUL FEELINGS

Recall the feeling you have when someone praises you, when you are approved, accepted, applauded. Now contrast that with the kind of feeling that arises within you when you look at the sunset or the sunrise—or nature in general—or when you read a book or watch a movie that you thoroughly enjoy. Get the taste of this feeling and contrast it with the first, namely, the one that was generated within you when you were praised. The first type of feeling comes from self-glorification and self-promotion. It is a worldly feeling. The second type comes from self-fulfillment, which is a soul feeling.

Here is another contrast: Recall the feelings you have when you succeed—when you've made it, when you get to the top, when you win a game, a bet, or an argument. Now contrast those feelings with the feeling you get when you really enjoy the job you are doing. The feeling you have when you are absorbed in the action you're engaged in. Once again, notice the qualitative difference between the first and the second: the worldly feelings and the soul feeling.

Yet another contrast: Remember what you felt like when you had power. Remember when you were the boss, when people looked up to you and took orders from you, or when you were popular. Contrast that worldly feeling with the feeling of intimacy and companionship, the times you thoroughly enjoyed yourself with a friend or a group in which there was fun and laughter.

Once you've done that, consider the true nature of worldly feelings, namely, the feelings of self-promotion and self-glorification. They are not natural; they were invented by your society and your culture to make you productive and controllable. Those feelings don't produce the nourishment and happiness that comes about from contemplating nature, enjoying the company of friends, or loving your work. They were meant to produce thrills, excitement— and emptiness.

Observe yourself in the course of a day or a week and think how many actions and activities you engage in that are uncontaminated by the desire for these thrills and excitements that only produce emptiness—the desire for attention, approval, fame, popularity, success, or power.

Take a look at the people around you. Is there a single person among them who hasn't become addicted to those worldly feelings? Is there a single person who is not controlled by them, hungering for them, spending every minute of their waking life consciously or unconsciously seeking them? When you see this, you will understand how people attempt to gain the world and, in the process, lose their soul. For they live empty, soulless lives.

YOUR SAD HISTORY OF
SELF-IMPROVEMENT

Compare the serene and simple splendor of a rose in bloom with the tensions and restlessness of your life. The rose has a gift that you lack: It is perfectly content to be itself. It has not been programmed from birth, as you have been, to be dissatisfied with itself, so it doesn't have the slightest urge to be anything other than what it is. It possesses the artless grace and absence of inner conflict that among humans is only found in little children and mystics. Only the adult human being is able to be one thing and pretend to be another.

Think of the sad history of your self-improvement efforts—they either ended in disaster or they succeeded only at the cost of struggle and pain. You are always dissatisfied with yourself, always wanting to change yourself, always wanting more. So, you are full of violence and self-intolerance, which only grows with every effort that you make to change yourself. Thus, any change you achieve is inevitably accompanied by inner conflict.

Now suppose you stopped all efforts to change yourself and ended all self-dissatisfaction. Would you then be doomed to go to sleep at night having passively accepted everything in you and around you?

There is another choice besides laborious self-pushing, on the one hand, or stagnant acceptance, on the other. It is the way of self-understanding. It is far from easy because to understand what you are requires complete freedom from all desire to change what you are into something else.

Consider the attitude of a scientist who studies the habits of ants without the slightest desire to change them. He has no other aim. He's not attempting to train them or get anything out of them. He's interested in ants; he wants to learn as much as possible about them. That's his attitude.

The day you attain a posture like that, you will experience a miracle. You will change—effortlessly and correctly. Change will happen; you will not have to bring it about. If what you attempt is not to change yourself but to *observe* yourself—to study every one of your reactions to people and things without judgment, condemnation, or desire to reform yourself—your observations will be nonselective, comprehensive, never fixed on rigid conclusions, and always open and fresh from moment to moment. Then you will notice a marvelous thing happening within you: You will be flooded with the light of awareness. You will become transparent and transformed.

A Philosopher's Tale

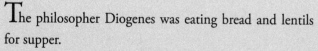

The philosopher Diogenes was eating bread and lentils for supper.

He was seen by the philosopher Aristippus, who lived comfortably by flattering the king.

Said Aristippus, "If you would learn to be subservient to the king, you would not have to live on lentils."

Said Diogenes, "Learn to live on lentils, and you will not have to cultivate the king."

The River Meditation

I look up at the sky and see the morning star
burn brightly in the heavens.
I imagine what it sees as it looks down
on me and my surroundings
and this portion of the earth.

I visualize what it must have seen
a thousand years ago . . .
five thousand . . .
a hundred thousand . . .
five million years ago.

I attempt to see in fantasy
what the morning star will see
in a thousand years . . .
five thousand . . .
a hundred thousand . . .
five million years from now
on the anniversary of this day.

I pass in review the various stages of my life—
infancy, childhood, adolescence,
adulthood, middle age—
in the following fashion:

I search for the things
that seemed immeasurably important
at each of these stages of my life,
things that caused me worry and anxiety,
things that I stubbornly clung to,
things that I thought I could never live with or without.

When I look back from the distance of today,
how many of those loves, dreams, and fears
retain the hold they had on me in former years?

Then I review
some of the problems that I have today,
some of my present suffering,
and of each of them, I say:
"This, too, will pass away."
I think of things I cling to
or that I am possessive of.
I realize that a day must surely come
when I shall see them differently.
So, of each of these attachments, too, I say,
"This, too, will pass away."

I make a list of the many things I fear,
and to each of them, I say,
"This, too, will pass away."

To end, I see myself embarking on my daily tasks
with the earnestness and fervor
with which I plunge into a drama
or a game,
absorbed, immersed, but never drowning.

PART TWO

HAPPINESS

"Take a look at the world
and see the unhappiness
around you and in you.
What causes this unhappiness?
You will probably say loneliness
or oppression or war
or hatred or atheism—
and you will be wrong.
There is only one cause of unhappiness—
the false beliefs you have
in your head."

What Is Happiness?

What, then, is happiness?

Very few people know. No one can tell you because happiness cannot be described. Can you describe light to people who have been sitting in darkness all their lives? Can you describe reality to someone in a dream? Understand your darkness, and it will vanish. Then you will know what light is. Understand your nightmare for what it is, and it will stop. Then you will wake up to reality. Understand your false beliefs, and they will drop. Then you will know the taste of happiness.

If people want happiness so badly, why don't they attempt to understand their false beliefs?

First, because it never occurs to them to see them as false or even as beliefs. They see them as facts and reality, so deeply have they been programmed. Second, because they are scared to lose the only world they know—the world of desires, attachments, fears, social pressures, tensions, ambitions, worries, and guilt with occasional flashes of pleasure and relief and excitement. It's like someone that is afraid to let go of a nightmare because, after all, it is the only world he knows. There you have a picture of yourself and of other people.

The Irony of Happiness

It's not possible to say that you are happy because the moment you become conscious of your happiness, you cease to be happy. What you call "the experience of happiness" is not happiness at all but the excitement and thrill caused by some person or thing or event. True happiness is uncaused. You are happy for no reason at all. True happiness cannot be experienced. It is not within the realm of consciousness. It is unselfconsciousness.

SEE THE UNHAPPINESS

Take a look at the world and see the unhappiness around you and in you. Do you know what causes this unhappiness? You will probably say loneliness or oppression or war or hatred or atheism—and you will be wrong. There is only one cause of unhappiness—the false beliefs you have in your head. These beliefs are so widespread and so commonly held that it never occurs to you to question them. It is because of these false beliefs that you see yourself and the world in a distorted way. Your programming is so strong and the pressure of society is so intense that you are literally trapped into perceiving the world in this distorted way. There is no way out, because you do not even have a suspicion that your perception is distorted, that your thinking is wrong, and that your beliefs are false.

Look around and see if you can find a single, genuinely, happy person, someone who is fearless and free from insecurities, anxieties, tensions, and worries. You would be lucky if you found one in a hundred thousand. This should lead you to be suspicious of the programming and the beliefs that you all hold in common. But you have also been programmed not to suspect, not to doubt, just to trust the assumptions that have been put into you by your tradition, your culture, your society, and your religion. And if you are not happy, you have been trained to blame yourself, not your programming and not your cultural and inherited ideas and beliefs. What makes it even worse is the fact that most people are so brainwashed that they do not even realize how unhappy they are—like a man in a dream who has no idea he is dreaming.

What Do You Have to Do to Get Happiness?

You don't have to do anything to acquire happiness because happiness cannot be acquired. Why? Because you have it already. How can you acquire what you already have? Uninterrupted happiness is uncaused. True happiness is uncaused. You cannot make me happy. You are not my happiness. You say to the awakened person, "Why are you happy?" and the awakened person replies, "Why not?" Happiness is our natural state. Happiness is the natural state of little children to whom the kingdom belongs until they have been polluted and contaminated by the stupidity of society and culture.

Then why aren't you experiencing happiness?

Because you've got to drop something. You've got to drop attachments. We were born happy. We lost it. We were born with the gift of life. We lost it. We've got to rediscover it. The world is full of sorrow. The root of sorrow is attachment, desire. The uprooting of sorrow is the dropping of attachment. The great Meister Eckhart said, "God is not attained by a process of addition to anything in the soul, but by a process of subtraction." You don't do anything to be free; you drop illusions. Then you're free. You don't have to add anything in order to be happy; you've got to drop attachments. Then you're happy.

How does one drop attachments? Through awareness. You only have to look and see that the attachment is based on a false belief that, without this, I cannot be happy. That's false; that's an illusion. The moment you see that belief is false, it drops, and you are free. That's what it is to watch yourself.

A Businessman's Tale

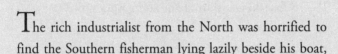

The rich industrialist from the North was horrified to find the Southern fisherman lying lazily beside his boat, smoking a pipe.

"Why aren't you out fishing?" said the industrialist.

"Because I have caught enough fish for the day," said the fisherman.

"Why don't you catch some more?"

"What would I do with it?"

"You could earn more money," was the reply. "With that, you could have a motor fixed to your boat and go into deeper waters and catch more fish. Then you would make enough to buy nylon nets. These would bring you more fish and more money. Soon you would have enough money to own two boats . . . maybe even a fleet of boats. Then you would be a rich man like me."

"What would I do then?"

"Then you could really enjoy life."

"What do you think I am doing right now?"

THE SECRET MEDITATION

I set out in search of the source
of the source of happiness.

I look minutely at the life
of a happy person who is poor,
then talk with him, attempting to discover
what makes this person happy.

I think of a joyful person in poor health,
in physical pain,
and talk again, searching for what it is
that makes her joyful.

I do the same with a happy person
who has lost his reputation.

I walk into a prison
and am amazed to find a happy person even here.
She tells me what it is
that makes her happy.

Then I observe unhappy people
who are free
and wealthy,
powerful,
respectable.
I talk to them,
and as they talk to me
I listen carefully to their complaints.

Yesterday I had occasions to be happy
that I wasn't even conscious of.
I see them now.

It is inconceivable that anyone
could be grateful and unhappy.
I thank the Lord for each event of yesterday
and notice the effect this has on me.

And the things I call unpleasant, undesirable
—I search for the good that comes from these . . .
the seeds for growth they carry . . .
and find reason to be grateful for them, too.

Finally I see myself
moving through each portion of today
in gratitude
—and happiness.

PART THREE

A GRACE CALLED AWARENESS

"Happiness is not an achievement;
love is not an achievement;
holiness is not an achievement;
it is a grace—
a grace called awareness,
a grace called looking,
observing,
understanding."

AWARENESS, AWARENESS, AWARENESS

There's a story about a disciple who went to the master and said, "Could you give me a word of wisdom? Could you tell me something that would guide me through my days?"

It was the master's Day of Silence, so he picked up a pad and wrote, "Awareness."

When the disciple saw it, he said, "This is too brief. Can you expand on it a bit?"

So the master took back the pad and wrote, "Awareness, awareness, awareness."

The disciple said, "Yes, but what does it mean?"

The master took back the pad and wrote, "Awareness, awareness, awareness means—awareness."

What you are aware of, you control. What you are unaware of controls you. You are always a slave to what you're not aware of. When you're aware of it, you're free from it. It's there, but you're not affected by it. You're not controlled by it; you're not enslaved by it. That's the difference.

When awareness is turned on, there's never any distraction, because you're always aware of whatever happens to be. No one can show you how to do it because he would be giving you a technique, he would be programming you. But watch yourself. When you were angry with somebody, were you aware that you were angry? Or were you simply identifying with your anger? Later, when you had the time, did you study your experience and attempt to understand it? Where did the anger come from? What brought it on? You only change what you understand and are aware of. What you do not understand and are not aware of, you repress. You don't change. But when you understand it, it changes.

Look at a person or a thing you have an attachment to. This is someone or something to whom you have handed over the power to make you happy or unhappy. Notice that—because of your concentration on getting this person or thing and holding on to it and enjoying it exclusively—you did so to the exclusion of other things and persons. See how—because of your obsession with this person or thing—you have less sensitivity to the rest of the world. You have become hardened. Have the courage to see how prejudiced and blind you have become in the presence of the object of your attachment. Allow that into your awareness. When you see that, you will feel a yearning to rid yourself of every attachment.

Renunciation and avoidance are of no help; to blot something out makes you as hard and insensitive as to obsess on it. What you need is not renunciation but understanding—awareness. If your attachments have caused you suffering and sorrow, that's a help to understanding. There is no substitute for the awareness that shows you the loss you suffer when you overvalue one thing to the exclusion of everything else. If, conversely, you have at least once in your life experienced the sweet taste of freedom and the delight in life that unattachment brings, that too is a help.

Looking, Observing, Understanding

Happiness is not an achievement; love is not an achievement; holiness is not an achievement. They are each a grace—grace called awareness, a grace called looking, observing, and understanding.

If you would only switch on the light of awareness and observe yourself and everything around you throughout the day; if you would see yourself reflected in the mirror of awareness the way you see your face reflected in a looking glass—accurately, clearly, exactly as it is without the slightest distortion or addition; and if you observed this reflection without any judgment or condemnation—for what you judge you cannot understand—you would experience all sorts of marvelous changes in yourself. You would not be in control of those changes, be able to plan them in advance, or decide how and when they are to take place. It is this nonjudgmental awareness alone that heals and changes and makes one grow. But it can only be done in its own way and at its own time.

AWARE OF WHAT?

What specifically are you to be aware of? Your reactions and your relationships. Each time you are in the presence of another person, with nature, or in any particular situation, you have all sorts of reactions, positive and negative.

Study those reactions, observe what they are and where they come from. Do so without any sermonizing or guilt or even any desire, much less effort to change them. That is all that one needs for holiness to arise.

But, you might ask, isn't awareness itself an effort? Not if you have tasted it even once. Once you have, you will understand that awareness is a delight; it is the delight of a little child moving out in wonder to discover the world. Even when awareness uncovers unpleasant things in you, it always brings liberation and joy. Then you will know that the unaware life is not worth living. It is too full of darkness and pain.

If at first there is a sluggishness in practicing awareness, don't force yourself. That would be an effort again. Just be aware of your sluggishness without any judgment or condemnation. You will then understand that awareness involves as much effort as a lover makes to go to her beloved, or a hungry man makes to eat his food, or a mountaineer to get to the top of his beloved mountain.

So much energy is expended, so much hardship even, but it isn't effort, it's fun! In other words, awareness is an effortless activity.

What I Mean by Awareness

An astronomer friend told me about some of the fundamental facts of astronomy. Until he told me, I didn't know that, when you see the sun, you're seeing it where it was eight and a half minutes ago, not where it is now. Because it takes a ray of the sun eight and a half minutes to get to us. So you're not seeing it where it is; it's now somewhere else. Stars, too, have been sending light to us for hundreds of thousands of years. So when we're looking at them, they might not be where we're seeing them; they might be somewhere else. He told me that, if we imagine a galaxy, a whole universe, this earth of ours would be lost toward the tail end of the Milky Way, not even in the center. Also, every one of the stars is a sun, and some suns are so big that they could contain the sun and the earth and the distance between them. At a conservative estimate, there are one hundred million galaxies! The universe, as we know it, is expanding at the rate of two million miles a second. I was fascinated listening to all of this, and when I came out of the restaurant where we were eating, I looked up at the night sky and had a different feel, a different perspective on life. That's awareness. You can pick all this up as cold fact. That's information. Or, suddenly, you can get another perspective on life. What are we? What's this universe? What's human life? When you get that feel, that's what I mean when I speak of awareness.

Come Home to Yourself

Observe yourself. Self-observation is such a delightful and extraordinary thing. After a while, you don't have to make any effort since, as illusions begin to crumble, you begin to know things that cannot be described. It's called happiness.

Would you rather live in darkness? Would you rather act and not be aware of your actions, talk and not be aware of your words? Would you rather listen to people and not be aware of what you're hearing or see things and not be aware of what you're looking at? The great Socrates said, "The unaware life is not worth living." That's a self-evident truth.

Most people don't live aware lives. They live mechanical lives, mechanical thoughts—generally somebody else's—mechanical emotions, mechanical actions, mechanical reactions. As you begin to understand this, you stop making demands on yourself, you stop having expectations of yourself, you stop pushing yourself, and you begin to understand yourself.

IF YOU'RE UNAWARE, YOU'RE VULNERABLE

If you aren't consciously aware, you're vulnerable to either being brainwashed or being influenced by forces within you that you have no awareness of at all. If you're aware of how you react to this book, for example, are you simultaneously aware of where your reaction is coming from? Maybe you are not taking in what you are reading at all. Maybe your mother or father is reacting to what I've written. Do you think that's possible? Of course it is.

Again and again in my therapy groups, I come across people who aren't there at all. Their daddy is there; their mommy is there; but they're not there. They never were there. "I live now, not I, but my daddy lives in me." Well, that's absolutely, literally true. I could take you apart piece by piece and ask, "Now, this sentence, does it come from Daddy, Mommy, Grandma, Grandpa? Whom?"

FOUR TRUTHS

If you want to reform your heart, you must give serious, prolonged thought to four liberating truths. Let's make an exercise of it. Choose some attachment that currently troubles you—something that you are clinging to, something that you dread, or something you are craving—and keep this attachment in mind as you read the following four truths.

The first truth: You must choose between your attachment and happiness. You cannot have both. The moment you pick up an attachment, your heart is thrown out of kilter and your ability to lead a joyful, carefree, serene life is destroyed. See how true this is when you apply it to your chosen attachment.

The second truth: Where did your attachment come from? You were not born with it. It sprang from a lie that your society and your culture have told you, or a lie that you have told yourself, namely, that without this or that, without this person or another, you can't be happy. Just open your eyes and see how false this is. There are hundreds of people who are perfectly happy without this thing or person or situation that you crave and that you have convinced yourself you cannot live without. So, make your choice: Do you want your attachment? Or do you want your freedom and happiness?

The third truth: If you wish to be fully alive, you must develop a sense of perspective. Life is infinitely greater than this trifle your heart is attached to, that which you have given the power to so upset you. Trifle, yes, because if you live long enough, a day will assuredly come when this thing will cease to matter. It will not even be remembered—your own experience will confirm this. Just as, today, you barely remember and are no longer the least bit affected by those tremendous trifles that so disturbed you in the past.

The fourth truth: The fourth truth brings you to the unavoidable conclusion that no thing or person outside of yourself has the power to make you happy or unhappy. Whether you are aware of it or not, it is you and only you who decides to be happy or unhappy—whether you choose to cling to your attachment or not to in any given situation.

As you ponder these truths, you may become aware that your heart is resisting them or that it argues against them and refuses to look at them. That is a sign that you have not yet suffered enough at the hand of your attachments to really want to do something about them. Or, your heart may have no resistance to these truths—if that is so, rejoice. Repentance, the refashioning of the heart, has begun. The Kingdom of God—the gratefully carefree life of children—has come within your grasp at last, and you are about to reach out and take possession of it.

FOUR STEPS

No event justifies a negative feeling. There is no situation in the world that justifies a negative feeling. Life is easy; life is delightful. It's only hard on your illusions, your ambitions, your greed, and your cravings. That's what all our mystics have been crying themselves hoarse to tell us. But nobody listens. The negative feeling is in you, not reality. It comes from your programming. The first thing you need to do is get in touch with negative feelings that you're not even aware of.

Almost every negative emotion you experience is the direct outcome of an attachment. So, there you are, loaded down by your attachments and striving desperately to attain happiness precisely by holding on to the load. It's absurd, but this is the only method that everyone has been taught for attaining happiness, yet it's a method guaranteed to produce anxiety, disappointment, and sorrow. Lots of people are depressed, and they're not aware they are depressed. It's only when they contact joy that they understand how depressed they were.

So, the first thing you need to do is to get in touch with negative feelings that you're not even aware that you have. What negative feelings? Gloominess, for instance. You're feeling gloomy and moody. You feel self-hatred or guilt. You feel that life is pointless, that it makes no sense. You've got hurt feelings, or you're feeling nervous and tense. Get in touch with those feelings first.

The second step is to understand that the feeling is in you, not in reality. That's such a self-evident thing, but do you think people know it?

The third step is to not identify with the negative feeling. Don't define your essential self in terms of that feeling. Don't say, "I am depressed." If you want to say, "My experience is depression" or "Depression is there," that's fine. If you want to say, "Gloominess is there," that's fine. But not, "I am gloomy." You're defining yourself in terms of the feeling. That's your illusion; that's your mistake. Don't define your essential self in terms of that feeling; the feeling does not affect the essential "I." It's similar to when you throw black paint in the air; the air remains uncontaminated. You never color the air black. No matter what happens to you, you remain uncontaminated.

So: there is a depression there right now, there are hurt feelings there right now, but let it be, leave it alone. It will pass. Everything passes. Everything. Your depressions and your thrills have nothing to do with happiness. Those are the swings of the pendulum. This has nothing to do with "I." The swings have nothing to do with happiness.

If you remember this, if you say it to yourself a thousand times, if you try these steps a thousand times, you will get it. You might not need to do it even three times. Step by step, let whatever happens happen. Real change will come when it is brought about—not by your ego, but by reality. Awareness releases reality to change you, but you have to experience it. Do it, and you'll make the biggest discovery in your life.

You Are Called Upon to Be Aware

A woman told me about two situations in which she found it difficult to be aware. She worked in social services where the phones were constantly ringing and clients were uptight and angry from having to stand in long lines. She found it extremely difficult to maintain serenity in that setting. The other situation in which she had difficulty maintaining peace of mind was driving in traffic. She was upset by horns blowing and people driving aggressively and shouting four-letter words. So, she asked me if her nervousness would dissipate eventually, and she'd be able to remain peaceful even in those situations.

Can you pick up the attachment there? Her attachment to being calm and at peace? She's essentially telling herself, "Unless I'm peaceful, I won't be happy." You don't make a goal out of relaxation and sensitivity. Have you ever heard of people who get tense trying to relax? If you are tense, you simply observe your tension.

You will never understand yourself if you seek to change yourself. The harder you try to change yourself, the worse it gets.

You are called upon to be aware. Get the feel of that jangling telephone; get the feel of jarred nerves; get the sensation of gripping the steering wheel tighter as your tension rises. In other words, come to reality and let the tension or the calmness take care of itself. As a matter of fact, you will have to let your mental state take care of itself because you'll be too preoccupied with getting in touch with reality.

Can You Be Happy
in Your Depression?

Did it ever occur to you that you could be happy in tension? Before enlightenment, I used to be depressed; after enlightenment, I continue to be depressed.

Step outside of yourself and look at that depression. Don't identify with it. Don't do a thing to make it go away; be perfectly willing to go on with your life while it passes through you and disappears. If you don't know what that means, you really have something to look forward to.

And anxiety?

Here it comes again, and you're not troubled. How strange! You're anxious, but you're not troubled. Isn't that a paradox? And you're willing to let this cloud come in because the more you fight it, the more power you give it. You're willing to observe it as it passes by. You can be happy in your anxiety. Isn't that crazy? You can be happy in your depression.

But you can't have the wrong notion of happiness. Did you think happiness was excitement or thrills? That's what causes the depression. Didn't anyone tell you that?

You're thrilled all right, but you're just preparing the way for your next depression. You're thrilled—but can you pick up the anxiety behind that? "How can I make it last?" That's not happiness; that's addiction.

Before enlightenment, I used to be depressed; after enlightenment, I continue to be depressed. But there's a difference: I don't identify with it anymore. Do you know what a big difference that is?

Two Sources for Change

Here is something else you must understand: There are two sources for change within you. One is the cunningness of your ego that pushes you into making efforts to become something other than you are meant to be—so that it can give itself a boost and glorify itself.

The other is the wisdom of nature. Thanks to this wisdom, you become aware, you understand it. That is all you do, leaving the type of change—the manner, the speed, the time of change—to reality and to nature. Your ego is a great technician, but it cannot be creative. It goes in for methods and techniques, and it produces so-called holy people who are rigid, consistent, mechanical, lifeless, and as intolerant of others as they are of themselves. They are violent people who are the very opposite of holiness and love. The type of "spiritual" people who, conscious of their spirituality, then proceed to crucify the Messiah.

Nature is not a technician. Nature is creative. You will be a creator, not a wily technician when there is abandonment in you—no greed, no ambition, no anxiety, no sense of striving, gaining, arriving, attaining. All you'll find is a keen, alert, penetrating, vigilant awareness that causes the dissolution of all one's foolishness and selfishness and all one's attachments and fears.

The changes that follow are not the result of your blueprints and efforts but the product of nature that spurns your plans and will, thereby, leave no room for a sense of merit or achievement or even any consciousness on the part of your left hand of what reality is doing by means of your right.

ACCEPTANCE AND PERSPECTIVE

This book is intended for busy people, active people, and energetic people. I'm not inculcating any mystical withdrawal from life—far from it. Christianity teaches that God and spirituality are to be found in life, not by withdrawing from them. There are two simple attitudes that help maintain spiritual awareness in everyday life for when some difficulty arises, as it always does.

The first attitude I call *acceptance*. It's contained in a prayer most of us have come to know, called the Serenity Prayer, which goes: God, grant me the grace to accept the things I cannot change, the courage to change the things I can, and the wisdom to know the difference. There are so many things in our lives that we cannot change. We're powerless, and if we learn to say Yes to these things, we will find peace because peace is found in Yes. You cannot change the ticking of the clock; you cannot change the death of a loved one; you cannot change the weather; you cannot change so many of your body's limitations and disabilities.

Now make an exercise of the things you cannot change. Stand before each one of them and say Yes, because, in doing that, you are saying Yes to God. If you find it difficult to do at times, then don't force yourself but, if you can find it in your heart to say Yes, understand that you are saying Yes to God's will, and, as the great

Italian poet Dante stated, "In His will is our peace." Nearly 95 percent of the things that upset our peace are things that we cannot change, and if you develop this attitude you will have peace, even in the things that you are fighting to change.

I call the second attitude *perspective*. What's that? Think of when you were a child and you clung to something so tenaciously that you did not want to give it up. You thought you would not be able to live without it. Think of some of the things that you detested and hated when you were a child or some of the things that you feared. How many of those fears and likes and dislikes persist still today? What happened to them? They passed away, did they not?

Make another list, this time of the things that you are possessive of, that you are dependent on, that you don't want to let go of. About each one of these things, say, "This, too, will pass away." Next, make a list of the things that you dislike and can't put up with. About each of those things, say, "This, too, will pass away." Now, make a list of your fears for the future and about each one of them say, "This, too, will pass away."

THE LITMUS TEST

As you use the sword of awareness to move from attachment into love, there is one thing you must keep in mind: Don't be harsh or impatient or hate yourself. How can love grow out of such attitudes? Instead, hold on to the compassion and the matter-of-factness with which the surgeon plies his knife. Then you may find yourself in the marvelous condition of loving the object of your attachment and enjoying it even more than before, yet simultaneously enjoying every other thing and every other person just as much. That is the litmus test for finding out if what you have is love.

Far from becoming indifferent, you now enjoy everything and everyone just as much as you did the object of your attachment, only now, there are no more thrills and therefore no more suffering and suspense. In fact, you could be said to be enjoying everything and enjoying nothing. Because you have made the great discovery that what you are enjoying on the occasion of each thing and person is something within yourself. The orchestra is within you, and you carry it with you wherever you go. The things and people outside you merely determine what particular melody the orchestra will play. And when there is no one or nothing that has your attention, the orchestra will play a music of its own; it needs no outside stimulation. You now carry in your heart a happiness that nothing outside of you can put there, and nothing can take away.

ANOTHER TEST

Here, then, is the other test of love. You are happy for no reason that you know of. But, does this love last? There is no guarantee that it does. For, while love cannot be partial, it can be of temporary duration. It comes and goes in the measure that your mind is awake and aware or has gone off to sleep again. But this much is certain: Once you have had even a fleeting taste of this thing called love, you will know that no price is too high, no sacrifice too great—not even the loss of one's eyes nor the amputation of one's hand—if you can have in exchange the only thing in the world that makes your life worthwhile.

NOTHING ELSE WILL
MATTER ANYMORE

Will awareness bring you the holiness you so desire? Yes and no. The fact is that you will never know. For true holiness—the type that is not achieved through techniques and efforts and repression—true holiness is completely unselfconscious. You wouldn't have the slightest awareness of its existence in you. Besides, you will not care, for even the ambition to be holy will have dropped away as you live from moment to moment in a life made full and happy and transparent through awareness. It is enough for you to be watchful and awake. For in this state, your eyes will see the Savior. Nothing else, but absolutely nothing else, will matter anymore. Not security, not love, not belonging, not beauty, not power, not holiness.

A Parable to Ponder

Here is a parable of life for you to ponder. A group of tourists sits in a bus that is passing through beautiful country, past lakes and mountains and green fields and rivers. But the window shades in the bus are pulled down. The passengers don't have the slightest idea about what lies outside the windows of the bus. The time of their journey is spent squabbling over who will have the seat of honor in the bus, who will be applauded, and who will be well considered. And so they remain until the journey's end.

What I'm leading you to is the awareness of reality around you. Awareness means to watch—to observe what is going on within you and around you. The term "going on" is pretty accurate: Trees, grass, flowers, animals, rock—all of reality is moving. One observes it; one watches it. It is essential for the human being not to just observe himself or herself, but to watch all of reality. Watch, observe, question, explore, and your mind will come alive, shed its fat, and become keen and alert and active. Your prison walls will come tumbling down until not one stone of the Temple will be left upon another. You will be blessed with the unimpeded vision of things as they are—the direct experience of Reality.

How sad it is if we pass through life and never see it through the eyes of a child. We need to return to paradise; we need to be redeemed again. We need to put off the old man, the old nature, the conditioned self, and return to the state of the child, but without being a child.

A Sufi's Tale

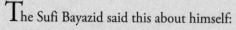

The Sufi Bayazid said this about himself:

I was a revolutionary when I was young, and all my prayer to God was, "Lord, give me the energy to change the world."

As I approached middle age and realized that half my life was gone without my changing a single soul, I changed my prayer to "Lord, give me the grace to change all those who come in contact with me—just my family and friends—and I shall be satisfied."

Now that I am an old man and my days are numbered, my one prayer is, "Lord, give me the grace to change myself."

If I had prayed for this right from the start, I should not have wasted my life.

THE ENLIGHTENMENT MEDITATION

When I try to change what I dislike in myself
by fighting it,
I merely push it underground.
If I accept it,
it will surface and evaporate.
What I resist will stubbornly persist.

I consider the example of Jesus,
who set himself the task of moving mountains
and battling with exasperating foes.
Yet, even in his anger, he is loving
—he combines a keen desire for change
with an acceptance of reality as it is.

I try to be like him.
I start with feelings I dislike.
To each of them, I talk
in a loving, accepting, kind way
and listen to what each has to say
till I discover that, while it can do me harm,
it also does me good,
that it is there for a benign purpose,
which I now attempt to see.

I keep on with the dialogue
until I feel a real acceptance of these feelings
—acceptance, not approval or resignation—
so that I am no longer depressed about my depressions,
angry over my anger,
or discouraged because of my discouragement,
or frightened of my fears
or rejecting of my feelings of rejection.
I can live with them in peace
for I have seen that God can use them for my good.

I do the same
with some of the many other things about my life
that I want to change:

My body's disabilities . . .

My personal shortcomings . . .

The external circumstances of my life . . .

The happenings of the past . . .

The people with whom I live . . .

The whole world as it is . . .

Old age, sickness, death.

I speak to them with love
and the consciousness that they somehow fit
into God's plan.

In doing so, I undergo a transformation:
while everything about me is the same
 —the world, my family, my feelings,
my body, my neuroses—

I am the same no longer.
I am more loving now,
more accepting of what is undesirable.
More peaceful, too,
for having come to see
that violence cannot lead to lasting change
—only love and understanding can.

Part Four

Who Am I?

*"The first quality that strikes one when one looks into
the eyes of a child is their innocence:
their lovely inability to lie or wear a mask or pretend
to be anything other than what they are.
Only an adult can be one thing and
pretend to be another."*

THE LION PARABLE

There's a famous story about the lion who came upon a flock of sheep and, to his amazement, found a lion among the sheep. It was a lion who had been brought up by the sheep ever since he was a cub. He would bleat like a sheep and run around like a sheep.

The lion went straight for him, and when the sheep-lion stood in front of the real one, he trembled in every limb. And the lion said to him, "What are you doing among these sheep?" And the sheep-lion said, "I am a sheep."

And the lion said, "Oh no you're not. You're coming with me."

So, he took the sheep-lion to a pool and said, "Look!" And when the sheep-lion looked at his reflection in the water, he let out a mighty roar, and in that moment he was transformed.

He was never the same again.

What Am I?

The great masters tell us that the most important question in the world is: "Who am I?" Or rather: "What is 'I'?"

What is this thing I call "I"? What is this thing I call myself?

You mean you understood everything else in the world, and you didn't understand this? You mean you understood astronomy and black holes and quasars, and you picked up computer science, and you don't know who you are? You are a sleeping scientist. You mean you understood what Jesus Christ is, and you don't know who you are?

My, you are still asleep.

How do you know that you have understood Jesus Christ? Who is the person doing the understanding? Find that out first. That's the foundation of everything, isn't it? It's because we haven't understood this that we've got all these stupid religious people involved in all these stupid religious wars. They don't know who they are. If they did, there wouldn't be wars.

WHO'S LIVING IN ME?

You think you are free, but there probably isn't a gesture, a thought, an emotion, an attitude, or a belief in you that isn't coming from someone else. Isn't that horrible? And you don't know it. A mechanical life has been stamped into you. You feel pretty strongly about certain things, and you think it is you who are feeling strongly about them, but are you really?

It's going to take a lot of awareness for you to understand that perhaps this thing you call "I" is simply a conglomeration of your past experiences, your conditioning, and your programming. That's painful. In fact, when you're beginning to awaken, you experience a great deal of pain. It's painful to see your illusions being shattered. Everything that you thought you had built up crumbles—and that's painful.

"I" Observing "Me"

Look at yourself as if you were watching another person, then write down on a piece of paper any brief way you would describe yourself. For example: businessman, priest, human being, Catholic, Jew. Anything.

Now, notice you've got "I" observing "me." This is an interesting phenomenon that has never ceased to cause wonder to philosophers, mystics, scientists, and psychologists. That the "I" can observe the "me." The great mystics of the East are really referring to that "I"—not to the "me." What constantly changes is "me."

What the "I" Is Not

Let's concern ourselves with something practical—deciding what the "I" is not. Am I my thoughts, the thoughts that I am thinking? No. Thoughts come and go; I am not my thoughts.

Am I my body? They tell us that millions of cells in our bodies are changed or are renewed every minute, and that by the end of seven years, we don't have a single living cell in our bodies that was there seven years before. Cells come and go. Cells arise and die—but "I" seems to persist. So am I my body? Evidently not!

"I" is something other and more than the body. You might say the body is part of "I," but it is a changing part. It keeps moving, it keeps changing. We have the same name for it but it constantly changes. Just as we have the same name for Niagara Falls, even though Niagara Falls is constituted by water that is constantly changing. We use the same name for an ever-changing reality.

How about my name? Is "I" my name? Evidently not, because I can change my name without changing the "I." How about my career? Not there either because I can change my career without changing the "I."

How about when I say, "I am successful." Is your success part of the "I"? No, successes are something that comes and goes; they could be here today and gone tomorrow. That's not "I." The same thing is true when you say, "I am a failure. I am a lawyer. I am a businessman."

How about my beliefs? I say I am a certain religion—is that an essential part of "I"? When I move from one religion to another, has the "I" changed? Do I have a new "I," or is it the same "I" that has changed? In other words, is my name an essential part of me, of the "I"? Is my religion an essential part of the "I"?

You're Not a Label

We spend so much of our lives reacting to labels, our own and others'. Christian and Muslim, Democrat and Republican, Communist and Capitalist. You know what's going to happen to you if you identify yourself with these things? You're going to cling to them; you're going to be worried that they might fall apart—and that's where your suffering comes in. We identify the labels with the "I." When you're caught up in labels, what value do these labels have, as far as the "I" is concerned? Could we say that "I" is none of the labels we attach to it? Labels belong to "me." What constantly changes is "me." Does "I" ever change? Does the observer ever change?

The fact is that whatever labels you think of (except perhaps "human being"), they should be applied to "me." "I" is none of these labels. When you step out of yourself and observe "me," you no longer identify with "me." Suffering exists in "me," so when you identify "I" with "me," suffering begins. When "I" does not identify with money, or name, or nationality, or persons, or friends, or any quality, the "I" is never threatened. It can be very active, but it isn't threatened.

Think of anything that caused or is causing you pain, worry, or anxiety. First, can you pick up the desire under that suffering—

that there's something you desire very keenly or else you wouldn't be suffering? What is that desire?

Second, it isn't simply a desire; there's an identification there. You have somehow said to yourself, "The well-being of 'I'—the existence of 'I'—is tied up with this desire."

All my suffering is caused by identifying myself with something, whether that something is within me or outside of me.

Someone once said, "The three most difficult things for a human being are not physical feats or intellectual achievements. They are, first, returning love for hate; second, including the excluded; third, admitting that you are wrong." But these are the easiest things in the world if you haven't identified with the "me."

You're Not a Concept Either

One reason we don't perceive people clearly is evident—our emotions get in the way, our conditioning, our likes and dislikes. We've got to grapple with that fact. But we've also got to grapple with some things that are much more fundamental—our ideas, our conclusions, our concepts. Believe it or not, every concept that was meant to help us get in touch with reality ends up by being a barrier to getting in touch with reality. That's because, sooner or later, we forget that the words are not the thing. The concept is not the same as the reality. They're different.

The final barrier to finding God is the word "God" itself and the concept of God. They can get in the way if you're not careful. They were meant to be a help; they can be a help, but they can also be a barrier.

When I give you a concept, I give you something, and yet how little I have given you. For instance, if I say that everyone in a room full of people is an animal, that would be perfectly accurate from a scientific viewpoint. But we're something more than animals.

If I say that Mary Jane is an animal, that's true, but because I've omitted something essential about her, it's false, and it does her an injustice. When I call a person a "woman," that's true, but there are lots of things in that person that don't fit into the concept "woman."

She is always this particular, concrete, unique woman, who can only be experienced, not conceptualized. This concrete person I've got to see for myself, to experience for myself, to intuit for myself. The individual can be intuited but cannot be conceptualized.

SELF-WORTH

Where do you get self-worth from? Do you get it from success in your work? Do you get it from having a lot of money? Do you get it from attracting a lot of men if you're a woman or a lot of women if you're a man?

How fragile all that is, how transitory. When we talk about self-worth, are we not talking, really, about how we are reflected in the mirrors of other people's minds? But do we need to depend on that?

One understands one's personal worth when one no longer identifies or defines one's self in terms of these transient things. I'm not beautiful because everyone says I'm beautiful. I'm really neither beautiful nor ugly. These are things that come and go. I could be suddenly transformed into a very ugly creature tomorrow, but it is still "I." Then, say I get plastic surgery, and I become beautiful again. Does the "I" really become beautiful? You need to give time to reflect on these things.

Our Lost Innocence

The first quality that strikes one when one looks into the eyes of a child is their innocence: their lovely inability to lie or wear a mask or pretend to be anything other than what they are. In this way, the child is exactly like the rest of nature. A dog is a dog; a rose, a rose; a star, a star; everything is quite simply what it is. Only an adult can be one thing and pretend to be another.

When grownups punish a child for telling the truth or revealing what it thinks and feels, the child learns to dissemble, and its innocence is destroyed. Soon, it will join the ranks of the numberless people who helplessly say, "I do not know who I am," for, having hidden the truth about themselves from others for so long, they end up by hiding it from themselves, as well.

How much of the innocence of childhood do you still retain? Is there anyone today in whose presence you can be simply and totally yourself, as nakedly open and innocent as a child?

There is another more subtle way in which the innocence of childhood is lost: when the child is infected by the desire to become somebody. Contemplate the crowds of people who are striving might and main to become, not what nature intended them to be—musicians, cooks, mechanics, carpenters, gardeners, inventors, artists—but *somebody*: successful, famous, powerful, something that will bring, not quiet self-fulfillment but self-glorification or self-expansion.

You are looking at people who have lost their innocence because they have chosen not to be themselves but to promote themselves, to show off, even if it is only in their own eyes. Look at your daily life. Is there a single thought, word, or action untainted by the desire to become somebody—even if all you seek to become is a spiritual success or a saint, unknown to anyone except yourself?

The child, like the innocent animal, surrenders to its nature to be and to become quite simply what it is. Adults who have preserved their innocence also surrender, like the child, to the impulse of nature or destiny without a thought to become somebody or to impress others. But, unlike the child, they rely, not on instinct but on ceaseless awareness of everything in them and around them. That awareness shields them from evil and brings about the growth that was intended for them by nature, not designed by their ambitious egos.

If you are not among the fortunate people with a fully actualized heart, you will have to do something to develop this heart of yours. There is nothing you can do directly. All you can do is silence your monkey mind and leave the heart to develop by itself.

Mystics and Children

The moment you make the child a carbon copy, you stamp out the spark of originality with which it came into the world. The moment you choose to become like someone else, however great or holy, you have prostituted your being. Think sadly of the divine spark of uniqueness that lies within you, buried under layers of fear—the fear that you will be ridiculed or rejected if you dare to be yourself and refuse to conform mechanically in the way you dress and act and think.

See how you conform not only in your actions and thoughts but even in your reactions, your emotions, your attitudes, and your values. You dare not break out of this prostitution and reclaim your original innocence. This is the price you pay for the passport of acceptance by your society or organization. So, you enter the world of the crooked and the controlled and are exiled from the kingdom that belongs to the innocence of childhood.

One subtle way you destroy your innocence is when you compete and compare yourself with others. When you do that, you exchange your simplicity for the ambition of wanting to be as good as someone else or even better.

Think of this: The reason why the child is able to preserve its innocence and live like the rest of creation in the bliss of the kingdom is that it has not been sucked into what we call "*the world*"—that region of darkness inhabited by grownups whose lives are spent not in living but in courting applause and admiration, not in blissfully being themselves but in neurotically comparing, competing, and striving for those empty things called success and fame—even if they can be attained only at the expense of defeating, humiliating, or destroying their neighbors.

If you allow yourself to really feel the pains of this hell on earth, the utter emptiness it brings, you might experience within you a revolt, a disgust so powerful that it will shatter the chains of dependence and deceit that have been forged around your soul, and you will break loose into the kingdom of innocence where mystics and children dwell.

TO WALK ALONE

To walk alone. That means to walk away from every formula—the ones given to you by others, the ones you learned from books, the ones that you yourself invented in the light of your own past experience. That is possibly the most terrifying thing a human being can do: move into the unknown unprotected by any formula.

To walk away from the world of human beings as the prophets and the mystics did is not to walk away from the company of those humans but from their formulas. Then, even though you are surrounded by people, you are truly and utterly alone. What an awesome solitude! That solitude, that aloneness, is Silence. It is only this Silence that you will see. And the moment you see, you will abandon every book and guide and guru. What is it that you will see?

Anything. Everything. A falling leaf, the behavior of a friend, the ripples on the surface of a lake, a pile of stones, a ruined building, a crowded street, a starry sky, whatever. After you have seen, someone may attempt to help you put your vision into words, but you will shake your head. "No, not that. That's just another formula."

Someone else will attempt to explain the meaning of what you saw, and you will shake your head again because meaning is a formula. Meaning is something that can be put into concepts and makes sense to the thinking mind, yet what you saw is beyond all formula, all meaning.

And a strange change will come about in you, barely perceptible at first but radically transforming. Because, having seen, you will never be the same again. You will feel the exhilarating freedom, the extraordinary confidence that comes from knowing that every formula, no matter how sacred, is worthless, and you will never again call anyone your teacher.

Then you will never cease to learn, as each day you will observe and understand afresh the whole process and movement of life. Then every single thing will be your teacher.

So, put your books and formulas aside, dare to abandon your teacher, whoever your teacher may be, and see things for yourself. Dare to look at everything around you without fear and without formula, and it won't be long before you see.

A King, a Queen

If you're lucky and the gods are gracious, or if you are gifted with Divine Grace—use any theological expression you want—you might suddenly understand who "I" is, and, like the lion in the parable, you'll never be the same again. Never.

Nothing will ever be able to touch you again, and no one will ever be able to hurt you again. You will fear no one, and you will fear nothing. Isn't that extraordinary?

You'll live like a king, like a queen. This is what it means to live like royalty. Not rubbish like getting your picture in the newspapers or having a lot of money. That's a lot of rot. You fear no one because you're perfectly content to be nobody. You don't give a damn about success or failure. They mean nothing. Honor, disgrace—they mean nothing! If you make a fool of yourself, that means nothing either. Isn't that a wonderful state to be in!

A Farmyard Tale

A man found an eagle's egg and put it in the nest of a backyard hen. The eaglet hatched with the brood of chicks and grew up with them.

All his life, the eagle did what the backyard chickens did, thinking he was a backyard chicken. He scratched the earth for worms and insects. He clucked and cackled. And he would thrash his wings and fly a few feet into the air.

Years passed, and the eagle grew very old. One day, he saw a magnificent bird far above him in the cloudless sky. It glided in graceful majesty among the powerful wind currents, with scarcely a beat of its strong golden wings.

The old eagle looked up in awe.

"Who's that?" he asked.

"That's the eagle, the king of the birds," said his neighbor. "He belongs to the sky. We belong to the earth—we're chickens."

So the eagle lived and died a chicken, for that's what he thought he was.

The Exposure Meditation

I think of the times I come alive
and the times when I am dead.

I ponder on the features I assume
in moments of aliveness
and in times when I am dead.

Life abhors security:
for life means taking risks,
exposing self to danger,
even death.
Jesus says that those who wish to be safe will lose their lives;
those who are prepared to lose their lives will keep them.

I think of the times
when I drew back from taking risks,
when I was comfortable and safe:
those were times when I stagnated.

I think of other times
when I dared to take a chance,
to make mistakes,
to be a failure
and a fool,
to be criticized by others,
when I dared to risk being hurt
and to cause pain to others.
I was alive!
Life is for the gambler.
The coward dies.

Life is at variance with my perception
of what is good and bad:
these things are good and to be sought;
these others bad and to be shunned.
To eat of the Tree of Knowing Good and Bad
is to fall from paradise.
I must learn to accept whatever life may bring,
pleasure and pain, sorrow and joy.
For if I close myself to pain
my capacity for pleasure dies
—I harden myself

and repress what I regard as unpleasant and undesirable,
and in that hardness, that repression,
is rigidity and death.

So I decide to taste in all its fullness
the experience of the present moment,
calling no experience good or bad.
Those experiences that I dread—I think of them,
and, inasmuch as I am able, I let them come
and stop resisting them.

Life goes hand in hand with change.
What does not change is dead.
I think of people who are fossils.
I think of times when I was fossilized:
no change, no newness,
the same old worn-out concepts
and patterns of behavior,
the same mentality, neuroses,
habits, prejudices.

Dead people have a built-in fear of change.
What changes have there been in me
over the past six months?
What changes will there be today?

I end this exercise
by watching nature all around me:
so flexible,
so flowing,
so fragile,
insecure,
exposed to death
—and so alive!

I watch for many minutes.

PART FIVE

THE KINGDOM OF LOVE

*"The finest act of love
you can perform is
not an act of service
but an act of
contemplation, of seeing.
When you serve people,
you help, support, comfort,
alleviate pain.
When you see them in their
inner beauty and goodness,
you transform and create."*

WHAT IS LOVE?

What is love? God's kingdom is love. It is a sensitivity to every portion of reality within you and without along with a whole-hearted response to that reality. It means to be sensitive to life, to things, to persons; it means to feel for everything and everyone to the exclusion of nothing and no one. Sometimes you will embrace that reality, sometimes you will attack it, sometimes you will ignore it, and other times, you will give it your fullest attention. But, always, you will respond—not from need but from sensitivity.

It is said that love is blind. But, is it? Actually, nothing on earth is as clear-sighted as love. The thing that is blind is not love but attachment. And what is attachment? Again, it is a need, a clinging that blunts your sensitivity, a drug that clouds your perception. That is why, as long as you have the slightest attachment for anything or any person, love cannot be born. For love is sensitivity, and sensitivity that is impaired even in the slightest degree is sensitivity destroyed. One must brave the stormy seas of attachments if one is to arrive at the land of love.

All or Nothing

Love, like sensitivity, either is in all its fullness or it simply is not. You either have it whole or you have it not. So, it is only when attachments disappear that one enters the boundless realm of spiritual freedom called "love."

You can hardly be said to love what you do not even notice. And, if you notice only a few beings to the exclusion of others, that is not love at all. For love excludes no one at all; it embraces the whole of life. Exclusion can only be achieved through a hardening of oneself, through closing one's doors. And the moment there is a hardening, sensitivity dies. It won't be hard for you to find examples of this kind of sensitivity in your life.

Have you ever stopped to remove a stone or a nail from the road to prevent someone from coming to harm? It doesn't matter that you will never know the person who will benefit from the gesture or that you will receive no reward or recognition. You just do it from a feeling of benevolence and kindness. Or, have you felt pained at the wanton destruction in another part of the world, of a forest that you will never see and never benefit from?

Have you gone to some trouble to help a stranger find his way although you do not know and will never meet this person again, purely from a goodheartedness that you feel within you? In these and so many other moments, love came to the surface in your life, signaling that it was there within you waiting to be released. How can you come to possess this kind of love? You cannot, because it is already there within you. All you have to do is remove the blocks you place to sensitivity, and it would surface.

BLOCKS TO LOVE

There are three blocks to love's sensitivity: belief, attachment, and fear. The first is belief. As soon as you have a belief you have concluded about a person or situation or thing, you have now become fixed and have dropped your sensitivity. You are prejudiced and will see the person through the eyes of that prejudice. In other words, you will cease to see the person again. And how can you be sensitive to someone you do not even see? Take just one or two of your acquaintances and list the many positive or negative conclusions you have arrived at about them, and on the basis of which you relate to them. The moment you say So-and-So is wise or cruel or defensive or loving, or whatever, you have hardened your perception and become prejudiced. You have ceased to perceive this person moment by moment, somewhat like a pilot who operates today with last week's weather report.

Take a hard look at these beliefs, for the mere realization that they are beliefs, conclusions, and prejudices and not reflections of reality will cause them to drop.

The second block is attachment. When you have a full-blown attachment, with it comes an inevitable exclusion of other things, an insensitivity to anything that isn't part of your attachment. Each time you leave the object of your attachment, you leave your heart there, so you cannot invest it in the next place you go. The symphony of life moves on, but you keep looking back, clinging to a few bars of the melody, blocking your ears to the rest of the music, thereby producing disharmony and conflict between what life is offering you and what you are clinging to.

Then comes the third block, fear, which is the tension and anxiety that are the very death of love and the joyful freedom that love brings. For love and freedom are only found when one enjoys each note as it arises, then allows it to go, so as to be fully receptive to the notes that follow.

TRUE LOVE?

It is commonly held that only when you feel deeply loved, you are able to go out in love to others. This is not true. A man in love does indeed go out to the world—not in love but in euphoria. For him the world takes on an unreal, rosy hue, which it loses the moment the euphoria dies. His so-called love is generated, not by his clear perception of reality but by the conviction, true or false, that he is loved by someone. It is a conviction that is dangerously fragile because it is founded on the unreliable, changeable people who he believes love him, and who can, at any moment, pull the switch and turn off his euphoria. No wonder those who walk this path never really lose their insecurity. Someone else controls the switch, and, when it is switched off, the glow fades away.

THE ROLLER COASTER RIDE

Left to its own devices, life would never produce love. Left to its own devices, life would only lead you to attraction, from attraction to pleasure, then to attachment, to satisfaction, which would finally lead to wearisomeness and boredom. After that would come a plateau. Then once again, the weary cycle: attraction, pleasure, attachment, fulfillment, satisfaction, boredom. All of this mixed with the anxieties, the jealousies, the possessiveness, the sorrow, and the pain that make the cycle a roller coaster.

When you have repeatedly gone around and around the cycle, a time finally comes when you have had enough and want to call a halt to the whole process. And if you are lucky enough not to run into something or someone else that catches your eye, you will have at least attained a fragile peace.

The Finest Act of Love

It is a sobering thought that the finest act of love you can perform is not an act of service but an act of contemplation, of seeing. When you serve people, you help, support, comfort, and alleviate pain. When you see them in their inner beauty and goodness, you transform and create.

Think of some of the people you like and who are drawn to you. Now attempt to look at each of them as if you were seeing them for the first time, not allowing yourself to be influenced by your past knowledge or experience of them, whether good or bad. Look for things in them that you may have missed because of familiarity, for familiarity breeds staleness, blindness, and boredom. You cannot love what you cannot see afresh. You cannot love what you are not constantly discovering anew.

Having done this, move on now to people you dislike. First, observe what it is in them that you dislike, study their defects impartially and with detachment. That means you cannot use labels like "proud," "lazy," "selfish," "arrogant." The label is an act of mental laziness, for it is easy to stick a label onto someone. It is difficult and challenging to see the person in their uniqueness.

You must study those defects clinically. That means you must first make sure of your objectivity. Consider the possibility that what you see as a defect in them may not be a defect at all but something that your upbringing and conditioning have led you to dislike.

If, after this, you still see a defect there, understand that the origin of the defect lies in childhood experiences, past conditionings, faulty thinking, perception, and, above all, in unawareness—not in malice. As you do this, your attitude will change into love and forgiveness, for to study, to observe, and to understand is to forgive.

Having made this study of defects, now search for the treasures buried in this person that your dislike prevented you from seeing before. As you do this, observe any change of attitude or feeling that comes over you, for your dislike has clouded the vision and prevented you from seeing. You can now move on to each of the people you live and work with, observing how each of them becomes transformed in your eyes when you look at them in this way. By seeing them in this way, it is an infinitely more loving gift that you offer them than any act of service. For you have transformed them, you have created them in your heart and given a certain amount of contact between you and them. They will be transformed in reality, too.

Now, make this same gift to yourself. If you have been able to do it for others, this should be fairly easy. Follow the same procedure: No defect, no neurosis is judged or condemned. You have not judged others; you will be amazed now that you yourself are not being judged. Those defects are probed, studied, and analyzed for a better understanding that leads to love and forgiveness. And, to your joy, you will discover that you are being transformed by this strangely loving attitude that arises within you toward this thing you call yourself—an attitude that arises within you and moves out through you to every living creature.

WHAT WILL SAVE THE WORLD

We think the world would be saved if only we could generate larger quantities of goodwill and tolerance. That's false. What will save the world is not goodwill and tolerance but clear thinking. Of what use is tolerance of others if you are convinced that you are right and everyone who disagrees with you is wrong? That isn't tolerance but condescension; it leads not to union of hearts but to division because you are one up and the others, one down. It is a position that can only lead to a sense of superiority on your part and resentment on your neighbor's, thereby breeding further intolerance.

True tolerance only arises from a keen awareness of the abysmal ignorance of everyone as far as truth is concerned. For truth is essentially mystery. The mind can sense it but cannot grasp it, much less formulate it. Life is a mystery, which means your thinking mind cannot make sense out of it. Our beliefs can point to it but cannot put it into words. In spite of this, people talk glowingly about the value of dialogue, which, at worst, is a camouflaged attempt to convince the other person of the rightness of your position, and which, at best, will prevent you from becoming a frog in the well who thinks that his well is the only world there is. What happens when frogs from different wells assemble to dialogue about their convictions and experiences? Their horizons widen to include the existence of wells other than their own. But they still have no suspicion of the existence of the ocean of truth that cannot be confined within the walls of conceptual wells. And our poor frogs continue to be divided and to speak in terms of "yours" and "mine": your experience, your convictions, your ideology, and mine. The sharing of formulas does not enrich the sharers, for formulas, like the walls of wells, divide. Only the unrestricted ocean unites. But to arrive at the ocean of truth that is unbounded by formulas, it is essential to have the gift of clear thinking.

WHAT IS CLEAR THINKING?

What is clear thinking and how does one arrive at it?

The first thing you must know is that it does not call for any great learning. It is so simple as to be within the reach of a ten-year-old child. What is needed is not learning but unlearning, not talent but courage.

You will understand this if you think of a little child in the arms of an old, disfigured housemaid. The child is too young to have picked up the prejudices of its elders. So, when it snuggles in that woman's arms, it is responding not to labels in its head—labels like "white woman," "black woman," "ugly," "pretty," "old," "young," "mother," "servant maid." It is responding, not to labels such as these but to reality.

That woman meets the child's need for love, and that is the reality the child responds to, not the woman's name and figure and religion and race and sect. Those are totally and absolutely irrelevant. The child has as yet no beliefs and no prejudices.

This is the environment within which clear thinking can occur. To achieve it, one must drop everything one has learned and achieve the mind of the child that is innocent of past experiences and programming that cloud our way of looking at reality.

Look into yourself, examine your reactions to persons and situations, and you will be appalled to discover the prejudiced thinking behind your reactions. It is almost never the concrete reality of this person or thing that you are responding to. You are responding to principles, ideologies, belief systems, economic, political, religious, psychological belief systems, and preconceived ideas and prejudices, whether positive or negative.

Take them one at a time—each person and thing and situation—and search for your bias separating the reality that's before you from your programmed perceptions and your projections. If you do this exercise, it will afford you a revelation as divine as any that the Scriptures could provide you with.

CHARITY

Charity is really self-interest masquerading as altruism. I'll have to explain that. There are two types of selfishness. The first type is the one where I give myself the pleasure of pleasing myself. That's what we generally call self-centeredness. The second is when I give myself the pleasure of pleasing others. That would be a more refined kind of selfishness. The first one is very obvious, but the second one is hidden, and for that reason, rather sinister, because we get to feel that we're really great. But maybe we're not all that great after all.

Think of someone who lives alone and goes to a hospital to volunteer several hours of her time. She readily admits she's really doing so for a selfish reason—she needs to be needed—and she also knows she needs to be needed in a way that makes her feel like she's contributing to the world a little bit. She sees that it's a two-way street. "I give something, I get something. My left hand had no idea what my right hand was doing." A good is never so good as when you have no awareness that you're doing good. As the Sufis say, "A saint is one until he or she knows it." Unselfconscious! Unselfconscious!

Some people do things so that they won't have to have a bad feeling—and they call it charity. They act out of guilt. That isn't love. If I had a dollar for every time I did things that gave me a bad feeling, I'd be a millionaire by now. You know how it goes. "Could I meet you tonight, Father De Mello? Something's upsetting me." "Yes, come on in!" I say. I don't want to meet him. I want to watch that TV show tonight. It doesn't give me a good feeling to meet with him, but it doesn't give me a good feeling to say *no* either, so I choose the lesser of the two evils and say, "Come on in." All the while, I'm thinking that I'm going to be happy when this thing is over and I'll be able to take my smile off.

That's the worst kind of charity, when you're doing something so you won't get a bad feeling. Charity is never so lovely as when one has lost consciousness that one is practicing charity.

CREATING A LOVING WORLD

When you are in love, you find yourself looking at everyone with new eyes. You become generous, forgiving, and kindhearted, where before you might have been hard and mean. Inevitably, people begin reacting to you in the same way and soon you find yourself living in a loving world that you yourself have created.

Or think of the time you were in a bad mood and found yourself becoming irritable, mean, suspicious, even paranoid. The next thing you knew everyone was reacting to you in a negative way and you found yourself living in a hostile world created by your head and your emotions.

How could you go about creating a happy, loving, peaceful world? By learning a simple, beautiful, but painful art called "the art of looking." This is how you do it. Every time you find yourself irritated or angry with someone, the one to look at is not that person but yourself. The question to ask is not "What's wrong with this person?" but "What does this irritation tell me about myself?" Do this right now. Think of some irritating person you know and say this painful but liberating sentence to yourself: "The cause of my irritation is not in this person but in me."

Having said that, begin the task of finding out how you are causing the irritation.

First look into the very real possibility that the reason why this person's defects or so-called defects annoy you is that you have them yourself, but you have repressed them and so are projecting them unconsciously onto the other. This is almost always true but hardly anyone recognizes it. So, search for this person's defects in your own heart and in your unconscious mind, and your annoyance will turn to gratitude that his or her behavior has led you to self-discovery.

Here is something else worth looking at: Can it be that you are annoyed at what this person says or does because those words and behaviors are pointing out something in your life and in yourself that you are refusing to see?

Think how irritated you get with the mystic and the prophet who look far from mystical to you when you are challenged by their words or their life. Another thing is also clear: You become irritated with this person because he or she is not living up to the expectations that have been programmed into you. Maybe you have a right to demand that he or she lives up to your programming, as for instance, when he or she is cruel or unjust. But then stop to consider this: If you seek to change this person or to stop this person's behavior, won't you be more effective if you were *not* irritated? Irritation will only cloud your perception and make your action less effective. Everyone knows that when a sportsman or a boxer loses his temper, the quality of his play goes down because it becomes uncoordinated through passion and anger.

In most cases, however, you have no right to demand that the person live up to your expectations; someone else in your place might be exposed to the same behavior and experience no annoyance at all. Just contemplate this truth, and your irritation will vanish. How foolish of you to demand that someone else lives up to standards and norms that your parents programmed into you!

And here is a final truth for you to consider: Given their background, life experience, and unawareness, they cannot help but behave the way they do. It has been so well said that to understand all is to forgive all. If you really understood the person, you would see him as crippled—not blameworthy—and your irritation would instantly cease. And the next thing you know, you'll be treating them with love, and they are responding with love, and you'll find yourself living in a loving world that you have yourself created.

BEHOLD YOUR SAVIOR

Jesus said, "Love your enemies. Do good to those who hate you."

How do we do that? Think of someone you dislike, someone you generally avoid because their presence generates negative feelings in you. Imagine yourself in that person's presence now and watch the negative emotions arise. You are, quite conceivably, in the presence of someone who is poor, crippled, blind, or lame.

Now understand that if you invite this person, this beggar, to come in from the streets and alleys, into your home, that is, into your presence, they will make you a gift that none of your charming, pleasant friends can make you, rich as they are. They are going to reveal yourself to you and reveal human nature to you. What this beggar is going to bring will widen your heart until there is room in it for every living creature. Can there be a finer gift than that?

Now take a look at yourself reacting negatively and ask yourself the following question: "Am I in charge of this situation, or is this situation in charge of me?" That is the first revelation. With it comes the second: The way to be in charge of the situation is to be in charge of yourself, which you are not. How does one achieve this mastery? All you have to do is understand that there are people in the world who, if they were in your place, would not be negatively affected by the person. They would be in charge of the situation, above it, not subject to it as you are. Therefore, your negative feelings are caused, not by this person, as you mistakenly think, but by your programming. That is the third and major revelation. See what happens when you really understand it.

Having received these revelations about yourself, listen to the revelation concerning human nature. The behavior, the trait in the other person that causes you to react negatively—do you realize that they are not responsible for it? You can hold on to your negative feelings only when you mistakenly believe that they are free and aware and therefore responsible. But whoever did evil in awareness? The ability to do evil or to be evil is not freedom but a sickness for it implies a lack of consciousness and sensitivity. Those who are truly free cannot sin as God cannot sin. This poor person in front of you is crippled, blind, lame, not stubborn and malicious as you so foolishly thought. Understand this truth; look at it steadfastly and deeply; and you will see your negative emotions turn into gentleness and compassion. Suddenly you have room in your heart for someone who was consigned to the streets and alleys by others and by you.

Now you will realize that this beggar came to your home with alms for you—for the widening of your heart in compassion and the release of your spirit in freedom. Where before you used to be controlled—this person had the power to create negative emotions in you and you went out of your way to avoid them—now you have the gift of the freedom to avoid no one and to go anywhere. When you see this, you will notice how the feelings of compassion and gratitude for this beggar, who is your benefactor, have been added to your heart. And another new, unaccustomed feeling: You actually feel a desire to seek out the company of these growth-producing crippled, blind, and lame people the way someone who has learned to swim seeks water. That's because each time you are with them, you can now actually feel an ever-expanding compassion and the freedom of the skies, where before you would feel the oppression and tyranny of negative feelings. And you can barely recognize yourself as you go out into the streets and alleys of the town, in obedience to the master's injunction, to bring in the poor, the crippled, the blind, and the lame.

A Worshiper's Tale

———◆———

There was once a woman who was religious and devout and filled with love for God. Each morning she would go to church and, on her way, children would call out to her, beggars would accost her, but so immersed was she in her devotions that she did not even see them.

Now one day she walked down the street in her customary manner and arrived at the church just in time for service. She pushed the door, but it would not open. She pushed it again, harder, and found the door was locked.

Distressed at the thought that she would miss service for the first time in years and not knowing what to do, she looked up. And there, right before her face, she found a note pinned to the door.

It said, "I'm out there!"

• • •

The disciple was always complaining to his master, "You are hiding the final secret of Zen from me!" He would not accept the master's denials. One day, they were walking in the hills when they heard a bird sing.

"Did you hear that bird sing?" said the master.

"Yes," said the disciple.

"Well, now you know that I have hidden nothing from you."

"Yes."

The Wellsprings Meditation

I seek the sources of refreshment,
sustenance, and healing
that my spirit, like my body,
is constantly in need of.

I am made whole again
 —my Self is given back to me—
in solitude and *silence*.

So now I seek to silence word and thought
by being conscious of the sounds around me,
or the sensations of my body,
or my breathing.

I am energized by *love*.

So I recapture
and relive
the times when I felt loved,
cared for, and treasured.

And I see myself going out in love
to friends,
to those who are in need,
and to every living creature.
I come alive in times of creativity.

How does it find expression in my life?

I get peace and *healing*
from my roots in nature.

I recall what happens when I am in harmony
with earth and sky,
with mountains, rivers, oceans
and nature's many moods
and nature's seasons.

I find everything in *prayer*,
which for me is fragrance and food,
a home, a shield, a tonic.
I recall the seasons of my prayer:
the moments I cry out in despair,
the days of glad thanksgiving,
the times of stillness,
presence,
adoration.

And I recite a prayer or song or poem
that I have come to love,
that I wish to have beside me all through life
and shall want my lips to say when I am dying.

PART SIX

UNION WITH GOD

*"If you are ever
to come to union
with God,
you must pass
through silence."*

A Finger Pointing to the Moon

You are surrounded by God, yet you don't see God because you "know" about God.

The final barrier to the vision of God is your God concept. You miss God because you think you know. That's the terrible thing about religion. That's what the gospels were saying that religious people "knew," so they got rid of Jesus. The great Chinese sage, Lao-Tse, said, "The one who knows, does not say; the one who says, does not know."

All revelations, however divine, are never any more than a finger pointing to the moon. As it is said in the East, "When the sage points to the moon, all the idiot sees is the finger."

The highest knowledge of God is to know God as unknowable. There is far too much God talk; the world is sick of it. There is too little awareness, too little love, too little happiness, but let's not use those words either. There's too little dropping of illusions, dropping of errors, dropping of attachments and cruelty, too little awareness.

That's what the world is suffering from, not from a lack of religion. Religion is supposed to be about a lack of awareness, of waking up. Look what we've degenerated into. Come to my country, India, and see them killing one another over religion. You'll find it everywhere.

Your Mystical Heart

Mystics tell us that, in addition to the mind and heart with which we ordinarily communicate with God, we are, all of us, endowed with a mystical mind and mystical heart. These are faculties that make it possible for us to know God directly, to grasp and intuit Him in His very being, though in a dark manner, apart from all thoughts and concepts and images.

Ordinarily, all of our contact with God is indirect—through images and concepts that necessarily distort His reality.

To be able to grasp God beyond these thoughts and images is the privilege of this faculty which I shall call the Heart, though it has nothing to do with our physical heart or our affectivity.

In most of us, this Heart lies dormant and undeveloped. If it were to be awakened, it would be constantly straining toward God and, given a chance, would impel the whole of our being toward God.

But for this, it needs to be developed, it needs to have the dross that surrounds it removed so that it can be attracted toward the Eternal Magnet.

The dross is the vast number of thoughts and words and images that we constantly interpose between ourselves and God when we are communicating with Him. Words sometimes serve to impede rather than foster communication and intimacy.

Silence—of words and thoughts—can sometimes be the most powerful form of communication and union when hearts are full of love. Our communication with God, however, is not quite so simple a matter. I can gaze lovingly into the eyes of an intimate friend and communicate with him beyond words. But what do I gaze into when I gaze silently at God? An imageless, formless reality. A blank!

Now that is just what is demanded of some people if they would go deep into communion with the Infinite, with God: gaze for hours at a blank. Some mystics recommend that we gaze at this blank lovingly. And it requires a good deal of faith to gaze with love and yearning at what seems like just nothing when we first get in touch with it.

If your mind isn't silenced, you will never even get anywhere near this blank, even supposing an intense desire on your part to spend hours on end gazing at it. As long as your mind machine keeps spinning out millions of thoughts and words, your mystical mind, or Heart, will remain underdeveloped.

The Riches of Silence

"Silence is the great revelation," said Lao-Tse. And so it is. I want you now to discover the revelation that silence brings. To take in the revelation that Scripture offers, you must expose yourself to Scripture. To take in the revelation that silence offers, you must first attain silence. And that is not easy.

Let us attempt to do this.

Take a comfortable posture. Close your eyes. I am now going to invite you to keep silence for a period of ten minutes.

First you will try to attain silence, as total a silence as possible of heart and mind.

Having attained it, you will expose yourself to whatever revelation it brings.

At the end of ten minutes, you can return to this page to read on.

The experience of people who attempt this exercise is infinitely varied. Most people discover, to their surprise, that silence is something they are simply not accustomed to. That no matter what they do they cannot still the constant wandering of their mind or quieten an emotional turmoil they feel within their heart.

Others feel themselves approaching the frontiers of silence. Then they panic and withdraw. Silence can be a frightening experience. No reason to be discouraged. Even those wandering thoughts of yours are a great revelation, aren't they? The fact that your mind wanders, isn't that a revelation about yourself? It is not enough to know this. You must take time to experience this wandering mind. And the type of wandering it indulges in—how revealing that is, too!

And here's something encouraging for you: The fact that you were aware of your mental wanderings or your inner turmoil or your inability to be still shows that you have some small degree of silence within you, at least a sufficient amount of silence to be aware of all of it.

Close your eyes again and become aware of your wandering mind for just two minutes. This time sense the silence that makes it possible for you to be aware of the wanderings of your mind.

At the end of two minutes you can return to this page to read on.

It is this minimal silence that you have within you that you can build on in the exercises in my book *Sadhana*. As it grows, it will reveal to you more and more about yourself. Or, more accurately, silence will reveal yourself to you.

That is the first revelation silence brings: your Self. And in and through this revelation, you will attain things that money cannot buy, things like wisdom and serenity and joy and God. To attain these priceless things, it is not enough for you to reflect, talk, discuss. What you will need is work.

Get to work right now. Close your eyes. Seek silence for another five minutes. At the end of the exercise, note whether your attempts this time are more successful or less. Note whether silence revealed something to you this time that you failed to notice last time.

Don't seek for anything sensational in the revelation that silence brings—lights, inspirations, insights. In fact, don't seek at all. Limit yourself to observing. Just take in everything that comes to your awareness, everything that is thus revealed to you, no matter how trite and ordinary. All your revelation might consist of is the fact that your hands are clammy or that you have an urge to change your posture or that you are worried about your health. No matter. The important thing is that you have become aware of this. The content of your awareness is less important than the quality of the awareness. As the quality improves, your silence will deepen. And as your silence deepens, you will experience change.

And you will discover, to your delight, that revelation is not knowledge. Revelation is power, a mysterious power, that brings transformation.

BREATHING AS A FORM OF PRAYER

Prayer is an exercise that brings fulfillment and satisfaction and it is perfectly legitimate to seek these from prayer. It is to be made less with the head than with the heart. In fact, the sooner it gets away from the head and from thinking, the more enjoyable and the more profitable it is likely to become. Most priests and religions equate prayer with thinking. That is their downfall.

A Jesuit friend once told me that he approached a Hindu guru for initiation in the art of prayer. The guru said to him, "Concentrate on your breathing."

My friend proceeded to do just that for about five minutes. Then the guru said, "The air you breathe is God. You are breathing God in and out. Become aware of that and stay with that awareness."

My friend followed these instructions—for hours on end, day after day—and discovered, to his amazement, that prayer can be as simple a matter as breathing in and out. And he discovered in this exercise a depth and satisfaction and spiritual nourishment that he hadn't found in the many, many hours he had devoted to prayer over a period of many years.

SILENCE

If you ever come to union with God, you must pass through silence. Any way to God must be a way through silence. Silence means going beyond words and thoughts. The first thing you need to do to attain the silence that reaches God is to realize that your ideas of God are all inadequate. God isn't anything you think or imagine. God cannot be described. For example, suppose that I'd never smelled a rose before, and I asked you what the fragrance of a rose smelled like. Could you describe it for me? Of course not.

Well, if you cannot describe a simple thing like the fragrance of the rose, how could you describe the Almighty? Whatever words you would use would fall short. Any image that your mind makes will be more unlike God than like God. The experience of God is totally beyond description or imagination. So, the first thing to acknowledge is that your ideas of God are all inadequate.

The second thing you need to do if you want to attain silence is simply look, listen, hear, and see. That's all you need to do. Let me explain that.

Mystics say that God dances the world. Think of a dancer and her dance. Each is not the same as the other, and yet neither are they divided in two. In truth, they are one. A great theologian once said that God is in creation the way the voice of a singer is in a song. But we miss this, don't we? For example, suppose I were to sing "Nearer, My God, to Thee." You've got my voice, you've got the song, and both are so intimately connected. Imagine that you are listening to the song, but you don't hear the voice. Imagine that you are looking at the dance, but you don't see the dancer. It is strange to think of seeing the dance but not recognizing the dancer, and yet that is exactly what happens when we go looking for God.

Imagine that I am looking at a sunset, enraptured, and a man comes to me and says, "You seem so enthralled. What are you looking at?"

I answer, "I'm overtaken by beauty."

And the man says, "I want that feeling, too." So he comes every day at evening to that spot to look for beauty. He looks and looks and he can see the sun, he can see the colors and the shimmering of light on the water, but not beauty.

"Where is beauty?" he demands. "Where?" He doesn't realize that beauty isn't a thing. He doesn't understand that beauty is a way of looking at things.

"It is only with the heart that one sees rightly," says the fox to the prince in the book *The Little Prince*. "What is essential," the fox says, "is invisible to the eye."

That is what you need; you need heart-hearing, heart-seeing for union with God, not words. The Gospel says, "He was in the world, for the world was created by Him, but the world did not recognize Him." Look at creation; just look. Don't look at ideas, look at creation itself. Just observe and become quiet.

Hopefully it will be given to you through grace that, as you look, silence will overtake you and then you will see. Look at the dance and hopefully you will recognize the dancer. If you would look, maybe you will recognize.

A Hasidic's Tale

———◆———

The Jews of a small town in Russia were eagerly awaiting the arrival of a rabbi. It was going to be a rare event, so they spent a lot of time preparing the questions they were going to put to the holy man. When he finally arrived and they met with him in the town hall, he could sense the tension in the atmosphere as all prepared to listen to the answers he had for them.

He said nothing at first; he just gazed into their eyes and hummed a haunting melody. Soon everyone began to hum. He started to sing and they sang along with him. He swayed and danced in solemn, measured steps. The congregation followed suit. Soon they became so involved in the dance, so absorbed in its movements that they were lost to everything else on earth; so every person in that crowd was made whole, was healed from the inner fragmentation that keeps us from the Truth.

It was nearly an hour before the dance slowed down to a halt. With the tension drained out of their inner being, everyone sat in the silent peace that pervaded the room.

Then the rabbi spoke the only words he pronounced that evening: "I trust that I have answered your questions."

• • •

A dervish was asked why he worshipped God through dance. "Because," he replied, "to worship God means to die to self; dancing kills the self. When the self dies, all problems die with it."

THE CARESS MEDITATION

Become aware of each sensation
on the surface of your skin,
beginning with the crown of your head
and moving downward to the tip of your toes.

It matters not that you feel no sensation
in some parts of your body.
The mere attempt to feel them
will give you the benefit of this exercise.

Now reflect that each sensation
is a biochemical reaction
that needs God's almighty power to exist.

Imagine you experience God's power
each time you experience these sensations.

Imagine each sensation to be a touch of God—
rough, smooth, pleasurable, painful.

Imagine this touch of God to be luminous
and healing.

PART SEVEN

SUFFERING
AND GROWTH

*"Suffering occurs when
you clash with reality.
When your illusions
clash with reality,
when your falsehoods
clash with truth,
then you have suffering.
Otherwise there is
no suffering."*

IF YOU'RE SUFFERING, YOU'RE ASLEEP

Spirituality is about waking up.

Do you want a sign that you're asleep? Here it is: You're suffering. If you're suffering, you're asleep. Suffering is a sign that you're out of touch with the truth. Suffering is given to you that you might open your eyes to the truth, that you might understand that there's falsehood somewhere, just as physical pain is given to you so you will understand that there is disease or illness somewhere.

Suffering points out that there is falsehood somewhere. Suffering occurs when you clash with reality. When your illusions clash with reality, when your falsehoods clash with truth, then you have suffering. Otherwise there is no suffering.

When you said, "I am a success," you were in error—and you were plunged into darkness. You identified yourself with success. The same thing is true when you said, "I am a failure," or when you ascribed any label to yourself. You know what's going to happen to you if you identify yourself with these things. You're going to cling to them, you're going to be worried that they might fall apart, and that's where your suffering comes in.

PAINFUL EXPERIENCES
LEAD TO GROWTH

Another truth: Pleasant experiences make life delightful, but they don't lead to growth in themselves. What leads to growth is painful experiences. Suffering points out an area in you where you have not yet grown, where you need to grow and be transformed and change. If you knew how to use that suffering, oh, how you would grow.

For the time being, let's limit ourselves to psychological suffering, to all those negative emotions we have. The disappointment you experience when things don't turn out as you wanted them to—watch that! Look at what it says about you, without condemnation, otherwise you're going to get caught in self-hatred. Observe it as you would observe it in another person. Look at that disappointment, that depression you experience when you are criticized. What does that say about you? That worry, that anxiety, what does it say about you? Negative feelings, every negative feeling is useful for awareness, for understanding, for growth.

THE BRIGHT SIDE OF SUFFERING

Think of some of the painful events in your life. How many of them are you grateful for today? Because, thanks to them, you changed and grew. Here is a simple truth of life that most people never discover: Every painful event contains in itself a seed of growth and liberation.

Happy events make life delightful, but they do not lead to self-discovery and growth and freedom. That privilege is reserved to the things and persons and situations that cause us pain. In the light of this truth, return to your life now and take a look at one or another of the events that you are not grateful for. See if you can discover the potential for growth that they contain, that you were unaware of and therefore have failed to benefit from.

Now think of some recent event that caused you pain, that produced negative feelings in you. Whoever or whatever caused those feelings was your teacher because they revealed so much to you about yourself that you probably did not know. And they offered you an invitation and a challenge to self-understanding, self-discovery, and therefore to growth and life and freedom.

Try it now. Identify the negative feeling that this event aroused in you. Was it anxiety or insecurity? Jealousy or anger or guilt? What does that emotion say to you about yourself, your values, your way of perceiving the world and life, and, above all, your programming and conditioning?

If you succeed in discovering this, you will drop some illusion you have clung to until now. As you realize that it was caused by your programming and not by reality, you will change a distorted perception or correct a false belief or learn to distance yourself from your suffering. You will suddenly find that you are full of gratitude for those negative feelings and to that person or event that caused them.

Now take this one step further.

Look at everything that you think, feel, say, and do that you do not like in yourself. Your negative emotions, your defects, your handicaps, your errors, your attachments, and your neuroses. Your hang-ups, and, yes, even your sins. Can you see every one of them as a necessary part of your development, holding out a promise of growth and grace for you and others that would never have been there except for this thing that you so disliked?

And if you have caused pain and negative feelings in others, were you not at that moment a teacher to them, an instrument that offered them a seed for self-discovery and growth? Can you persist in this observation until you see all of this as a happy fault, a necessary sin that brings so much good to you and to the world?

A Guru's Tale

$\blacklozenge$

A disciple told his guru that he was going to a far place to meditate and hopefully attain enlightenment. So he sent the guru a note every six months to report the progress he was making.

The first report said, "Now I understand what it means to lose the self."

The guru tore up the note and threw it in the wastepaper basket.

After six months, he got another report, which said, "Now I have attained sensitivity to all beings." He tore it up.

Then a third report said, "Now I understand the secret of the one and the many." It too was torn up. And so it went on for years, until finally no reports came in.

After a time, the guru became curious, and one day there was a traveler going to that far place. The guru said, "Why don't you find out what happened to that fellow."

Finally, he got a note from his disciple. It said, "What does it matter?"

When the guru read that, he said, "He finally got it! He got it!"

The Dawn Meditation

Listen to nature waking up to greet the newborn day.
Notice the blending of silence and song in nature:
how varied are creation's songs,
how deep its silence!
None of nature's sounds
disturbs the eternal silence
that enfolds the universe.
If you listen to those sounds
you will someday hear the silence.

What sentiment do you think creation is expressing
as it wakes up,
as it replaces, with activity,
the quiet of the night?

Listen to your heart now.
There is a song there too,
for you are a part of nature.
If you have never heard the song,
you have not really listened.
Listen! What kind of song is it?
Sad . . . happy . . .
hopeful . . . loving?

There is also silence in your heart.
If you become aware
of each thought, each distraction,
each fantasy and feeling,
you cannot fail to sense that silence.

Now see your heart's song blending
with the song of nature all around you.

Listen.
The more sensitive your listening
the more silent you will be.
The more silent you become
the more sensitive will your listening be.

CONCLUSION

I Can Assure You of This

If we really dropped illusions for what they can give us or deprive us of, we would be alert. The consequences of not doing this are terrifying and inescapable. We lose our capacity to love. If you wish to love, you must learn to see again. And if you wish to see, you must learn to give up your drug. It's as simple as that. Give up your dependency.

Tear away the tentacles of society that have enveloped and suffocated your being. You must drop them. Externally, everything will go on as before, but though you will continue to be *in* the world, you will no longer be *of* it. In your heart, you will be free at last, if utterly alone. Your dependence on your drug will die. You don't have to go to the desert; you're right in the middle of people; you're enjoying them immensely. But they no longer have the power to make you happy or miserable. That's what aloneness means.

In this solitude, your dependence dies; the capacity to love is born. One no longer sees others as means of satisfying one's addiction. Can you imagine a life in which you refuse to enjoy or take pleasure in a single word of appreciation or to rest your head on anyone's shoulder for support? Think of a life in which you depend on no one emotionally, so that no one has the power to make you happy or miserable anymore. You refuse to *need* any particular person or to be special to anyone or to call anyone your own. The birds of the air have their nests, and the foxes their holes, but you will have nowhere to rest your head in your journey through life. If you ever get to this state, you will at last know what it means to see with a vision that is clear and unclouded by fear or desire. Every word there is measured. You will know what it means to love. But to come to the land of love, you must pass through the pains of death, for to love persons means to die to the need for persons, and to be utterly alone.

How would you ever get there? By a ceaseless awareness, by the infinite patience and compassion you would have for a drug addict. By developing a taste for the good things in life to counter the craving for your drug. What good things? The love of work which you enjoy doing for the love of itself; the love of laughter and intimacy with people to whom you do not cling and on whom you do not depend emotionally but whose company you enjoy. It will also help if you take on activities that you can do with your *whole being*—activities that you so love to do that while you're engaged in them success, recognition, and approval simply do not mean a thing to you.

It will help, too, if you return to nature. Send the crowds away, go up to the mountains, and silently commune with trees and flowers and animals and birds, with sea and clouds and sky and stars. I've said what a spiritual exercise it is to gaze at things, to be aware of things around you. Hopefully, the words will drop, the concepts will drop, and you will see, you will make contact with reality.

Be patient. Don't expect to do all of this in twenty-four hours. Some people are lucky; they seem to see it in a flash, and it makes all the difference to them. Others take time. But as the time goes, particularly if you listen with an open mind, things will become clearer by themselves.

I can assure you of this: Get started, and you will quickly see the results. The upsets will still keep coming, depending on the depth of the programming, but I'll promise you this: I have not known a single person who gave time to being aware who didn't see a difference in a matter of weeks. The quality of your life changes, so you don't have to take it on faith anymore. You see it; you're different. You react differently. In fact, you react less and act more. You are much more energetic, much more alive. You see things you've never seen before. For you have discovered what people everywhere are searching for and rarely find, namely, the fountainhead of serenity and joy that hides in every human heart.

Acknowledgments

We wish to thank Penguin Random House for permission to use material from the following books:

Excerpt(s) from WELLSPRINGS: A BOOK OF SPIRITUAL EXERCISES by Anthony De Mello, copyright © 1984 by Anthony de Mello, S. J.. Used by permission of Doubleday, an imprint of the Knopf Doubleday Publishing Group, a division of Penguin Random House LLC. All rights reserved.

Excerpt(s) from REDISCOVERING LIFE: AWAKEN TO REALITY by Anthony De Mello, copyright © 2012 by Center for Spiritual Exchange, Inc.. Used by permission of Image Books, an imprint of Random House, a division of Penguin Random House LLC. All rights reserved.

Excerpt(s) from AWARENESS by Anthony De Mello, copyright © 1990 by The Center for Spiritual Exchange. Used by permission of Doubleday, an imprint of the Knopf Doubleday Publishing Group, a division of Penguin Random House LLC. All rights reserved.

Excerpt(s) from THE WAY TO LOVE: THE LAST MEDITATIONS OF ANTHONY DE MELLO by Anthony De Mello, copyright © 1991 by Gujarat Sahitya Prakash of Anand, India. Used by permission of Doubleday, an imprint of the Knopf Doubleday Publishing Group, a division of Penguin Random House LLC. All rights reserved.